JUDITH COSBY

Spirit
Threads

Messages of hope and healing

Cover Design by Ana Grigoriu–Voicu, Books Design

Editing by Veronica Jorden, Storyteller Alley

Proofreading by Justine Murphy

Illustrations by Amanda Putnam

ISBN-13: 978-1-7341153-0-7 (print book)

ISBN-10: 1-7341153-0-0 (print book)

ISBN-13: 978-1-7341153-1-4 (e-book)

ISBN-10: 1-7341153-1-9 (e-book)

10 9 8 7 6 5 4 3 2 1

1. Spirituality 2. Self Help 3. Fox 4. Memoir 5. Inspiration 6. Supernatural 7. Empowerment

First Edition

Visit my website at www.judithcosby.com

"Extraordinary magic is woven through ordinary life. Look around!"

~ Amy Leigh Mercree

Table of Contents

Dedication

I dedicate this book to my family for their constant support and love.

To my husband, Craig, for his belief in my ability to write and his sweet acceptance of my rusty red friends.

To my daughters, Sarah and Catherine, for continuing to show me what strength, love, and hope really are.

To my mother, Shirley, for her loving support.

A special Thank you to the foxes, Reddy and Reddy Girl, for their messages of hope and their gifts of friendship.

Preface

When deciding to write this book I was unsure of how to continue the concept of my first book *Threads*. But, if there is one thing I have learned through the creation of *Threads*, it is that the story leads me rather than me leading it. Being open to that revelation has put me onto so many interesting paths.

After *Threads* was released, I was asked by many readers to share the story of my daughter Cate and me, and to be open about the journey of her illness and how we walked that path together. At first, I rejected the request to share our private journey because of the personal nature of the subject matter and how painful it was. I am, by nature, an empath and at times the sharing of these stories was so deeply painful I could not bear the thought of putting it all down on paper. It required a lot of strength, love, and faith to follow that road and I wasn't sure I could bring myself to relive all of the moments again.

The more I fought it, the more the readers asked. During these conversations, readers would often share their intimate pain with me about their loved ones. I began to realize that so many of us share the worry and hurt of loving someone who suffers. The most profound part was that I became acutely aware that it didn't matter what the infirmity was. That was irrelevant. What was glaringly apparent was that we all suffer in some form or another, and how we all gain hope by sharing our stories.

Cate's battle was with Chronic ITP, but I heard stories about family members who were suffering from diabetes, cancer, alcohol and/or drug addiction, depression, sexual abuse, and severe injuries due to an accident. Regardless of the infirmity, it became clear that we all feel the same hurt. Sharing our roads traveled gives each of us a voice, a way to cope and to not feel so alone.

When that epiphany broke through the walls of my resistance, I was able to sit down and write from the heart what it is like to walk such a difficult path. What it is like to be a caregiver, a cheerleader, a friend, a parent, a sounding board, and above all, how it feels to be someone who loves so deeply that they would give anything to end the pain of a loved one.

The journey Cate and I share has had so many ups and downs. Along the way, we have learned a valuable life lesson: embrace all of the good and all of the bad of each moment and learn from it. So, as *Spirit Threads* was born, I chose to dedicate this year of my life to those who shared their stories with me.

May you find this story and see it as a journey of hope.

Introduction

"Spring passes and one remembers one's innocence.
Summer passes and one remembers one's exuberance.
Autumn passes and one remembers one's reverence.
Winter passes and one remembers one's perseverance."

~ Yoko Ono

In my debut memoir *Threads*, I shared the concept of creating a grand tapestry composed of life lessons, each represented by a specific thread. It was this idea of creating and weaving a dynamic life that led me to share my story in memoir form. The original inspirational idea came to me during a church sermon when I was a young woman. That Sunday morning mass led me to a path of enlightenment and helped me pursue a life of positivity and openness. I began to envision my life in tapestry form, a form that provided clarity and the knowledge that I could alter the paths of my life in a more positive and loving way. Connections to people and places began to take on a deeper meaning, and I began to understand that they had been sent to me for a reason. I started to recognize that life itself could be a beautiful, intricately woven portrait, embroidered and stitched with even the simplest of moments as it spans into the vast universe to connect with others.

In any life, there are times that bring about more pain, more challenges, more growth, and more acceptance. They usually stem from a period of great trauma or massive flux and end with a stronger and more resilient mindset.

When I thought about how my life has evolved and transformed since I wrote *Threads*, I realized there were specific events that had added a greater depth and a richer essence to my picture; a year of what some might call misfortune and emotional upheaval. What I discovered amidst all of the trials of that period was that I had learned quite a bit about myself. And perhaps more importantly, finally figured out what I truly wanted out of life.

What evolved in that one year span of time was a change of heart for what I thought I had always desired. I had always imagined a life filled with excitement, adventure, and all of the expensive, shiny status symbols of success. But what I gleaned from living through that difficult time period was something purely simple and utterly life changing.

My new life objective had shifted from the desire for material things to simply this: appreciation and gratitude for the gift of an ordinary day.

To live simply, calmly, with normalcy and status quo is the gift of a wonderful life. I found that life held gems within the simplest of moments. Gratitude for good health, a happy home, and an appreciation for an ordinary day emerged within my being.

I share this year in my tapestry for a reason. Every stitch sewn brought about a profound change in how I defined a good and successful life. I was and am forever changed by this part of my life and although it was painful, it was also spirituality invigorating. I am grateful for the experience and the textures and colors it added to my tapestry.

Always reach for the stars and the moon, always fight for a vivacious life, but never underestimate the treasure and the pleasure of an ordinary day. Weave that into all of the fabric of your life.

1

The Threads of the Winter Weave

"There's just something beautiful about walking on snow that nobody else has walked on. It makes you believe you're special, even though you know you are not."

~ Carol Rifka Brunt

The Threads of New Meetings

It was late December and a snowstorm had raged through the night and left a blanket of snow about eight inches thick over the hilly terrain of our backyard. With the early dawn rising, the wind died down to a soft whisper. All that was left as the dim morning light emerged were the large white chunks of snow that fell from the sky in slushy, wet plops.

My husband, Craig, and I had a ritual of getting up at dawn and taking our dogs out for a walk before getting ready for work. On this particular day, we both had decided to call in as the roads were not completely plowed and salted. Our dogs, Maggie Mae, a Golden Retriever/Great Pyrenees mix, and Tobin, a Great Pyrenees, were used to our morning routine and anxiously waited for us at the bottom of the stairs.

We decided to remain in our routine and began the tedious task of dressing in our thick down coats, Sorel snow boots, and our wool hats and gloves. Craig wore a red and black flannel bomber hat with ear flaps and he suddenly resembled Nanook of the North.

"Love the hat!"

"Me too," he smirked. "It screams chick magnet, right?"

We fastened the dogs' lighted collars, snapped on their leashes, and stepped out onto the front landing. The air was crisp and the world was silent. The dawn was rising through thick, dark grey clouds, illuminating the downy, white ground.

We started our trek early enough that the salters, sanders, and plows had finished their work for a bit and their steely noises against the rutted pavement and beeping as they turned and maneuvered their way through our neighborhood had ceased. There was an impenetrable silence, like we were inside a giant snow globe, and the crunching of snow beneath our boots and paws was the only sound.

Maggie and Tobin loved the snow and so, for the first part of our walk, they hopped, played, licked, and dug in the wet, white mounds that covered the ground. But soon, they each needed to do their "business" and we separated into two sections of the neighborhood. The sky still cast a dim light as we trudged through the slush.

As Maggie and I passed a group of oak trees, I heard a strange screeching sound above us. It was so jarring that I looked up into the bare tree and scanned to see what could possibly be making that sound. Maggie stood erect for a moment, her pink nose pointed straight up into the air, sniffing hard and scanning the tree above.

A whizzing sound flew by my right shoulder and a soft splat hit the blanketed ground. I peered at the hole in the snowdrift. Maggie and I both stood still. To our horror, two long wriggling snake-shaped objects emerged from the hole, creating an almost alien-like visual and I screamed at the sight. How could a snake be out in winter, I thought? As I looked intently at the movement in the snow I realized that these objects were actually wet squirrel tails! As quickly as that thought left my mind, out of the tiny hole appeared a little grey head. A squirrel looked up at us with beady black eyes and started this loud chattering sound. It was a ghastly sight, to say the least.

Maggie, I believe, was just as stunned and did not make a move or a sound. Within seconds, a second grey head appeared, blankly staring at us both. There we were, all four of us, just staring at each other. Suddenly, one of the squirrels climbed out of the hole and gruffly grabbed the other, and dragged it back up the side of the oak tree.

It was then that I noticed that the pristine white ground was mired with blots of discoloration, bits of crimson stark against the snow within the trail of prints that they had left behind. I wondered if the squirrels had been injured from their fall. But then I observed more blood further up the path toward my house. I pulled Maggie away and called to my husband that we were heading home.

Once the dogs were settled in the house and the morning sun had climbed solidly above the horizon, I returned to the tiny blood trail to inspect the evidence and see if I could ascertain what might have happened. I bent over to examine the snow, my mind theorizing like I was a CSI agent at a crime scene. As I followed the trail, I noticed a lack of animal prints in the immediate area, which confused me. I had assumed it was attacked within this area, but maybe the squirrel was able to free itself from whatever attacked it.

Suddenly, directly above me, I heard the sound of cracking branches. Stunned by the noise, I looked up. What I could only assume was the same injured squirrel from before, fell from the tree and landed directly next to me, unquestionably dead.

I returned home to retrieve a shovel to bury the squirrel, perplexed by the timing and circumstances of the poor creature's death. Was it a fisher cat attack or possibly an owl? Did the squirrel get hit by a plow? That would have been odd since they don't typically start foraging for food until daylight. I came back to the spot a few minutes later with shovel in hand hoping to make quick work of this unpleasant task.

I knelt down and gently pushed the shovel under the tiny grey body and immediately felt in my gut the strange sensation of being watched. I stood, my breath forming a small cloud in the air from the bitter cold. I slowly turned to look into the woods behind my home.

I spied something hiding in the brush in the distance. I felt the stare from beyond the bramble, beyond the wood piles and barren trees. The faint silhouette of a fox watching me closely as I hovered over the dead squirrel took shape. It both startled and upset me that something wild was here harming our little wildlife.

The fox noticed me looking back at it and in a burst of rusty red, turned and ran through the thickly treed area that separated our neighborhood from the one behind us. This dense undergrowth led directly to a section of woods that rimmed the entire neighborhood.

That was the day I first met her—The fox that would be both a harbinger of the challenges to come and a symbol of hope and perseverance.

Looking back at our first encounter, I think I was instinctively and sensitively aware of the connection between us. The colored threads of her beautiful reddish brown fur and the intensity of those dark eyes had begun a weave between us that brought vibrancy and depth to a new section of my tapestry.

This fox and I had woven our first seams together and part of me knew it would be far from the last.

The Threads of Reality

It was during this same time period that my 24-year-old daughter, Catherine, or Cate, as we call her, was enjoying a period of remission in her battle with Chronic ITP. ITP, or Immune Thrombocytopenia Purpura, is a disease that can lead to easy or excessive bruising and bleeding. It is a condition characterized by a sudden and abnormal decrease in platelets. This destruction is due to the presence of antiplatelet autoantibodies. In other words, antibodies directed against the person's own cells. It is often defined as idiopathic because the cause is unknown.

For months, I could not pronounce the actual name, mainly because I think I hated it so much I chose not to. The acute form of the disease is usually temporary and treated with a steroid like Prednisone. In my daughter's case, it was chronic, and she fell into the 30 percent of patients who did not achieve remission through the normal avenues of treatment. It had been almost a year since her initial diagnosis in February 2017. A year filled with having to learn about her disease, of combating it with various treatments, some successful and some not so much. A year that included five hospitalizations and a reluctant but necessary acceptance of what her life had become.

Cate had been scheduled for an open splenectomy on October 12th and just days before her surgery both her surgeon at Brigham and

Women's Hospital and her oncologist hematologist at the Dana Farber Cancer Institute cancelled the procedure because her platelet count had been holding strong for weeks without medication. We all celebrated as if it was a miracle and that she had beat this thing. Those days in October were met with such jubilation for this victory.

What we did not anticipate was that after the decision was made to nix the surgery, she would then have to endure weekly blood draws to monitor her platelet count to make sure she remained stable. Those weekly blood draws were not just uncomfortable, they were also like a form of Russian roulette. We never knew what the outcome would be and if her nightmare would return. Those days were met with a certain level of angst and dread. If the numbers dropped even a little, we would all panic. If the results were positive, we celebrated with such gusto. And so, we danced this medical dance for almost two months, and then finally it was decided that she was a remission candidate.

It was as if life had finally given Cate the gift of good health. She had faced a difficult year battling every challenge thrown at her and after all these months she was enjoying a respite from it all.

At long last, we were given the gift of ordinary days.

Cate was amazing during this time of her life, so mature and forward-thinking. I was always in awe of her maturity and often wondered if I could have been as tough at her age. Even though the treatments and the emotions could be really draining, she never once waivered in her goal of remission and regaining her life. She had completed her degree and was now ready to find her place in the world.

She was currently interviewing for a recovery support specialist job and although the facility was an hour away, it was the dream job she had longed for. The interviewer seemed genuinely pleased to possibly have her on their team.

We were all excited about the upcoming Christmas holiday. Life it seemed had mellowed and we were in full celebration mode. Decorating, shopping, attending Christmas plays and parties. Amid all of the festivities, in early December, Cate noticed some bruising from time to time, but otherwise exhibited good health. A steady but slow feeling of fatigue would come and go, and at times wipe her out. But her now-monthly blood draws for her platelet count relayed positive numbers, and our family relished with jubilation the blessing of her good health.

Christmas week arrived with a whirlwind of joy and excitement and in our eyes, we had an extra thing to be grateful for. But the days right before Christmas seemed to bring another tone and tenor to our celebrations. Cate had begun to tire more easily; her gums began to bleed and her pale complexion had become waxy. On Christmas Eve, her bruising started to increase and her teeth, usually bright white, had a greyish tone to them.

I knew what this was.

I told Craig about my concern. He had sensed it too. Even my Mom noticed the change on Christmas Day and relayed her concerns to me. Cate, I think, already knew in her heart what was wrong, but chose not to let it ruin the holidays for her and her family.

I had told my mom I would be contacting the D'Amour Cancer Center in Springfield, MA and Dana Farber in Boston, MA first thing in the morning. Our Christmas Day celebrations went on as planned, but our hearts felt heavy and sad.

The next morning, I made my phone calls, but the majority of the staff we were accustomed to seeing had the week after Christmas off. Fortunately, Cate's main nurse at D'Amour Cancer Center was still on duty and we were able to get in contact with her oncologist hematologist at Dana Farber. They both agreed to have her go right to D'Amour Cancer Center lab for her blood draw, stat.

We waited for the results, praying for a miracle. When the results came in, the news delivered a mighty blow. Cate was in a platelet crash. Her body had only 1,000 platelets—far and dangerously below the normal range of 150,000 to 350,000. Her hematologist oncologist recommended an immediate platelet transfusion.

We spent the day after Christmas at the lab. They poured over 250,000 platelets into her frail body over a period of three hours.

I sat quietly watching my strong, beautiful girl as she so nonchalantly entered back into the fray. Cate sat on a gurney writing in her new journal, a Christmas present from Craig and me. She wore a pretty, white, Irish-knit sweater, jeans, suede boots with fringe hanging from them, and a new, grey, knitted hat with a faux-fur pom-pom on it. Her beautiful strawberry blonde hair flowed from under the hat and down her petite frame. Even fighting for her life, the girl could dress! She always looked so beautiful, no matter what was going on in her life.

As I looked at her, so calm and cool, I remembered the time she had to wear an EEG monitor on her head for three days. It was an ugly ecru-colored, knit head cover with electrodes attached to the sides of her head, forehead, and chest. She couldn't wash her hair and the glue they used on the electrodes pushed her hair up into clumps around her head. Most of us would have hidden from the world, but not Cate. She'd donned fresh makeup and put fresh flowers in sections of the mesh all over her head. She looked like a fashion model and I had to admire her defiance of this homely apparatus. She'd made that monitor more an accessory than a medical apparatus and she totally rocked that look.

The head lab nurse came into our cubicle to talk to Cate and it was hard not to notice the look of shock on her face. I introduced myself and she did the same. I read her face immediately as she apologized for her reaction.

"It is so nice to finally meet you, Catherine," she said offering her hand. "I've seen your platelet count come across my desk for over a year now, and it was not until this very moment that I realized how young you are! This whole time I assumed you were someone older!"

She continued, "But looking at you now, I realize you are just a baby."

Cate smiled and shook her hand. "Nice to meet you."

"We are working with a skeleton crew due to the holidays, but you should be fine to go home now," the nurse continued. "You will have to come back tomorrow for another blood draw."

Cate thanked her as she was unhooked for the IV stand and swung her legs over the edge of the bed. She smiled a half-hearted smile at Craig and me and jumped down onto the floor.

At least, for now, we knew she was safe.

We left and headed home to relax and wait.

The next morning came way too fast. Christmas was still spread across my house in opened presents under the tree, wrapping paper and bows stuffed in the trash barrel, and the scent of balsam and cedar wafting from our Yankee Candle jar, but the celebration itself seemed eons away.

We headed out early for another blood pull stat and possible transfusion. After waiting a few minutes, Cate's nurse came out with a concerned look on her face. Cate's body had basically massacred the innocent little platelets that had entered her body only 18 hours earlier. She was down to 5,000 platelets and there was no need for another platelet transfusion. Her body would just destroy them as quickly as she received them.

The realization that this was more dire than we had first thought began to hit us. A call was made into her oncologist hematologist at Dana Farber and an order for several days of IVIG infusions (intravenous immunoglobulin) was scheduled. IVIG is a blood product prepared from the serum of between 1,000 and 15,000 donors per batch. It is a treatment used for patients who suffer from antibody deficiencies and is a major go-to infusion for those who suffer from ITP. Cate would receive two days of infusions to get her through until she could be seen in Boston that Friday.

Cate sighed. "I hate IVIGs. They don't work for me and I always end up with the worst migraines."

I dreaded them too. It usually meant severe, debilitating headaches for Cate, no matter what the prepared medicinal cocktail they gave her to prevent them.

She seemed a tad defeated but was, as usual, a warrior going with the flow to get the job done. She wanted her life back and she wanted it back soon. It was December 27th and she was looking at starting her new job on January 2nd and did not want this to affect her goal.

Inwardly, I knew achieving that goal was going to be impossible. I could either tell her up front that it probably wasn't going to happen, or let her think it could, and then watch her suffer even more as another hope was crushed.

I chose to let her hope if for no other reason than to let the dwindling supply of holiday joy last just a bit longer.

The Threads of an Unexpected Messenger

Later that evening, after we returned from the hospital with Cate, I once again saw the fox in my yard. She was meandering along the edges, foraging in the brush and oblivious to my stare. I stood mesmerized by her, watching all of her nuances, and began to see things about her I had not noticed before. I recognized that she wasn't as red as I initially thought and that there was no white tip to her tail. And that I was beginning to be less edgy with her in my yard. Little by little, I was letting my guard down.

As the days progressed from the first sighting of the mysterious fox, she appeared more frequently. I do believe that by tossing bird seed and bread ends out for the birds and squirrels, that I inadvertently invited this foxy creature into my yard. She liked to forage in the brush at the edge of my property and dine on my bread ends and hunt. During those brief encounters, I witnessed the intensity of her eyes, particularly when they looked at me. Those impassioned eyes would actually peer right into mine with an innate "all knowing."

I did not know much about foxes in the beginning. All I knew was that I had a tiny wild beast that liked showing up in my yard at dusk and dawn and that would look straight at me and, well, she would smile.

But as the encounters increased, so did my knowledge about my new friend. I had always assumed that foxes were crafty and cunning animals. I did not know they would find a mate and breed in the winter months, between December and February, or that they were omnivores. Their diet varied, but could consist of bugs, fruit, seeds, grasses, or berries, as well as squirrels, mice, moles, rabbits, birds, and chipmunks. I did not know that between March and May they prepare a den for rearing their kits. But I was nothing if not curious and some online research also unlocked the mystery of why she remained near my property.

I had to admit, though, that I was drawn to her. For some reason I couldn't put words to, she reminded me a little of myself. She was a subtle creature to say the least, as she scurried about the woods and yards in my neighborhood. There was no level of flamboyance to her and she preferred to remain inconspicuous whenever she came to visit my yard.

But I couldn't deny the effect she had on me. With each appearance, she would mystically bestow a moment of both calm and foreboding upon me. It was a little unsettling sometimes.

Cate began the IVIG treatments but her numbers were not budging. Two days of the treatment did not bolster her failing platelets. Her latest platelet count went as low as zero. It became a frantic race to increase them. The treatment wasn't working and I felt as though we were all becoming a little unhinged.

Craig had taken the week off in advance of the holiday season so we were able to spend the majority of our time sitting with her during those long, tedious hours in the infusion rooms. I always admired my husband during these difficult times. He stayed so calm and would joke with her as they would share muffins and crackers or some other treat from the hospital vending machine. I was grateful for his strength during these moments so that I could react and assess things from a distance.

We had to face the fact that these treatments were not working. It was becoming increasingly difficult not to feel defeated and scared. The horror of what would happen if something didn't start working was real and I felt as if hope was ebbing away.

The final IVIG caused Cate to become so violently ill she couldn't lift her head and she began to vomit severely. By Friday morning, Cate had been in bed for over 24 hours and we had a scheduled appointment in Boston. I placed cold compresses on her head and dosed her with migraine meds in hopes that she would be able to make the drive. We prepared our car for the two-hour drive with blankets and buckets, praying that something would change in the next few hours. After several attempts to walk her to the car had failed, we brought her back into the house. She had become so weak that moving her would make her vomit profusely. Trying to make the appointment on our own was futile and we all knew it.

We made Cate as comfortable as we could on the couch and made the phone call.

I trembled with fear as I waited for the call to connect. I explained to her doctor at Dana Farber the dilemma we were in and he ordered a strong anti-nausea medicine. Craig immediately picked it up at our local pharmacy and she was dosed right away. But unfortunately it did not quell the nausea in time for our departure to Boston. We were left with no choice but to cancel the trip. Once again we contacted her doctor. Thankfully he recommended we do the appointment via a conference call in a few hours.

We all sat in our living room, the phone on speaker so we could all hear what the doctor had to say. Cate was awake with a cold cloth on her head and lying very still. The anti-nausea meds had finally started to kick in and she was able to gain a reprieve from the violent torture she dealt with that morning.

"I think we know where we are in this process," the doctor said. "Cate isn't responding to the classic treatments, so it's time we proceed with the next step—an open splenectomy. It has an excellent success rate, about 70 percent, and I feel that is where we should progress. Are we all on board?"

Cate nodded. Craig and I said, "Yes."

We were all so weary. This had been one hell of a week. Cate had been through so much. There was a sense of relief in knowing she still had a possible avenue to remission.

"Okay then," her doctor said. "I will have my administrative assistant start the process of booking the surgery ASAP and we will be contacting the surgeon immediately. I am stopping any further IVIG treatments and will have you start back on Nplate injections beginning next week."

Nplate (romiplostim) is a subcutaneous injection that helps increase platelet count. It must be administered weekly in order to keep the platelet counts up and consistent. It had worked initially for her in the latter part of the year but not consistently. Fingers crossed it would provide a temporary fix to get her to her surgical date.

We hung up the phone and all went into our personal corners to digest the news. I went to the kitchen and began to clean. Rinsing dishes, loading the dishwasher, and wiping the counters down in a compulsive fashion was my way of expending nervous energy. While cleaning, I would periodically stop and stare out the window into the backyard scanning for something, but unsure what. The entire ground was blanketed in snow and to me, everything looked dead and barren.

There was a flutter of activity over by my gazebo where the suet feeders hung. A red-bellied woodpecker and a hairy woodpecker were going to town eating the various types of suet nestled in the cages. Some of the seed I had placed in the bird feeders lay scattered all over the patio from the constant barrage of overzealous squirrels.

Tired from the week, and my mind in much need of a respite, the swaying of the ornamental grass tufts from a cold breeze and the melodic movement of the feeders as the birds had their fill put me in a trance. My mind wandered for just a minute to another place and time. Two little girls swam in a pool in the backyard yelling, "watch this momma, watch this," as they did acrobatics off their floats and landed with splashes in the clear, blue water.

Then as suddenly as the recesses of my mind played that memory of so long ago, I was abruptly brought back into the present.

I sighed. Hard.

Inhaling and exhaling.

I tried to keep the sobs that were just under the surface from breaking through my lips. I had gone back in time when my girls were little, healthy, and happy. When life was so easy and simple.

Then, something moved outside, and I froze.

On the barren brick patio was the fox. The reddish creature, more strawberry blonde than red, licked the melting ice from within the fire pit basin. She looked up into my window. I swore she could see me and did not care.

She moved down the patio steps to scrounge and dine on the remnants of fruit and seed mix that lay atop the snow. As she crunched on her treats, she would look nervously behind her and to her left and right as if she was wary of an attack, but mostly she looked up at me in the kitchen window.

I watched this wild creature moving about my patio, sniffing and eating. I tried to rationalize why she was out at this time of day. How bold and cunning! My dogs noticed her and started to bark ferociously through the atrium door window. She jumped and ran straight into the treed buffer zone and towards the woods.

I was mesmerized by her appearance and the timing of her arrival. She had silently entered into the yard like a specter from beyond the grave, emerging into my view and coming to me just when I needed her. It was as if I had beckoned her from somewhere deep inside and she heeded the call. Her presence soothed me and somehow encouraged me to let go of my doubt and redirect my thoughts. Whatever that moment was, my mind broke from its dark place, and I resumed a more positive mindset.

I looked down at the pool of water in my sink and the singular plate in my hand, wondering how long I had left the water to run.

The Threads of Preparation

After the conversation with Cate's oncologist hematologist, we prepared for a visit out to Dana Farber the following week, and then to her selected surgeon at Brigham and Women's Hospital.

Cate was nervous, but after meeting her surgeon, she understood why he came so highly recommended. He and his staff were awesome. With Cate's pre-op physical and surgical date booked, we returned home and tried to stay positive.

As a bleed risk, the doctor explained, an open splenectomy was the preferred method so that if something went wrong on the operating table, the doctor would be able to see everything right before him. In a laparoscopic splenectomy, if there is a bleed, she would immediately have to be flipped over and precious time could be lost.

Cate agreed, even knowing that it would leave her with a larger scar and a longer healing time.

The surgeon also explained how they would pump her body with Nplate to assure her platelet level would remain high for the actual surgery. They would prefer over 50,000 platelets to operate, but if need be, would perform the surgery as long as her numbers were above

25,000. She had been hovering in the 35,000 range, and I had become increasingly panicked.

During those weeks prior to her surgery, it all felt surreal. We booked our hotel, walking distance from Brigham and made our plans for our daughter, Sarah, to take care of our dogs, Maggie and Tobin, while we were away. Cate would be hospitalized for approximately a week and I wanted things in order while we were away. Her surgery was booked for 7:00 AM on February 12th so we made plans to stay in Boston the night before.

Now we just had to wait. We had a few weeks to mentally prepare for the long road ahead. I became increasingly anxious about the trip home after Cate's surgery. I was worried the two-hour ride home would be a painful one so I spent extra time planning how we were going to transport her with the least amount of discomfort.

In this midst of all of our planning and preparation, Craig and I continued to get up early and walk the dogs at dawn, trying to keep them on their schedule. It soon became apparent that on our daily walks we were being followed by the fox. At first, she stayed just inside the wood line. It was as if she was tracking us and I was more than a little confused about why she had no fear of my dogs, who together weighed about 175 pounds. Maggie and Tobin, were very sweet, but held a brute strength that could easily crush this fox that couldn't weigh more than 20 pounds.

We would spy her in the underbrush of the woods that rimmed the neighborhood and nearby wetlands. My husband suggested that I carry the pepper spray with us in the event of an unexpected attack. I had been reading up on foxes and learned a lot more about their habits. I wanted to understand why we were being hunted.

I read that when a fox trots, he puts his back left foot in the prints of his front right foot and his back right foot in the prints of his front left foot. In doing this strange walk, he is able to leave a straight line of prints from behind him! Clearly, I was dealing with a crafty beast or possibly just a really great dancer!

I also read that fox cubs are born in early March and won't emerge from the den until they are about four weeks old. The female is called a vixen and the male is called a dog fox. During the time when the kits are small and live within the den, the dog fox and vixen bring food for them to eat. As they get older, they fend for themselves, but often the parents will bring them an injured animal to hunt and kill so they can perfect their hunting skills. They also like to flatten grass down in a field or yard to lie down in, as I would witness many times in the upcoming summer months.

The fox also has very acute hearing, which was one of the things I had noticed when it came to its response to movements within my backyard. They have a short and deep warning bark that is similar to a dog's bark. I had actually heard that several times while in my yard and questioned what type of dog had made that bark and how close it often sounded within the perimeter of my yard. Although they appear shy and aloof, they are very skilled at hunting. They often come off as bold as they hunt and protect their young. All these small tidbits of information were giving me a clearer picture of what I was dealing with, and I did not feel as threatened as I had in the earlier days.

Then one morning while walking back through a wooded wetland area not far from our home I heard the sound of nails tapping on the pavement behind me. My husband and Tobin were about ten feet ahead of Maggie and me. I slowly turned, half expecting to find a wayward dog following us when I saw the fox trotting about 20 feet behind us! Her little lithe body was moving at a steady clip, mouth open, tongue showing, with the look of urgency in her eyes. In a slow motion reaction, I turned and yelled at my husband.

"Craig! Don't look back, just take Tobin and RUN!"

Apparently, in husband speak, that means, stop, turn, and stare at the Armageddon heading your way.

"Shit!" he yelled. Slowing the pace considerably and now only about a foot in front of Maggie and me, we almost collided and our leashes became entangled.

He now had a 105-pound Great-Pyrenees anchor dragging him down as Tobin twisted and turned barking at the fox.

"Holy hell, Craig!" I yelled, "I told you not to look back!"

Craig's face showed a sense of urgency as he tried to flank the rear with Tobin.

He yelled, "JUDE, RUN!"

We took off at a crazy pace, zig-zagging as the dogs pulled us one way and we pulled the other! We were banking one of us would be the weakest link as we were hunted by this tiny red beast.

Unfortunately for Maggie, I was the weakest! As we ran, dragging our furry anchors behind, I turned around to see if the fox was on my heels. I observed how she had slowed down, looking puzzled and actually bewildered at our insane response. The fox made an abrupt left into a neighbor's yard and ran through the woods.

I stopped, confused by her reaction. Was she showing aggression? It did not seem so. My God, did she think she was part of our pack? I continued to jog until we got to the front door. I stopped for a brief moment, leaned forward with both hands on my knees to catch my breath. Once inside, I unleashed Maggie and walked towards Craig with all the pent up anger I had.

"What the heck was that? I tell you to not look back and run and you do exactly the opposite!" I chastised.

"Well, you can't say stuff like that and not expect me to know what I am running away from!" Craig responded exasperated.

"That's ridiculous! We need a code word. We are being hunted and we need a word that means run without saying anything else." I said firmly.

Craig looked at me with skepticism in his face, but he knew better at that moment than to argue with me. The crazed look in my eyes was scarier than actually being hunted by a fox.

"Okay, how about "the shitter's full," Craig said with affirmation in his voice.

I stopped for a moment to process this suggestion.

"What the hell are you talking about? That is a phrase!" I said with frustration in my voice.

"What?" Craig said puzzled. "It's our mantra from 'Christmas Vacation,' you know, Cousin Eddy…"

I rolled my eyes and shook my head, but I pondered it for a just a moment and then thought it was brilliant.

"Why not?" I mused. It summed up this crazy situation perfectly.

"Okay, if this happens again, whoever says it, the other just runs."

"Agreed," Craig said with a nod.

And so, it went on. Often the walks kept us on high alert as our foxy friend skulked around from a distance. The dogs always knew where she was. They would literally sniff the air in large huffs and stand erect. Their tails would wag slightly.

One night she ran down the sidewalk with us and we switched sides, and then she ran back to our house and sat on the side yard waiting for our return! It was like a cat and mouse game and we were always the mouse, being outsmarted by this predator.

On another cold, bitter night, she followed our running steps to our front door. We barely made it through the entry as she closed in on our heels. Two adults and two large dogs pushing and shoving each other to get up the front stairs and into the safety of our house must have been a crazy sight. I began to think my dogs were enjoying the game too. It was fun to watch mommy and daddy run and squeal each time we walked.

This whole time, I puzzled over her trust that we would not let these two large beasts loose on her. But I believe she innately knew we would not, and therefore, could not contain herself from trying every single time to join our little pack.

A random "shitter's full" would be hollered out on various parts of our walk. I am sure if our neighbors heard us, they would indeed think one of us had a form of Tourette's. But after a while, the code phrase was no longer necessary. It became apparent that the fox was more interested in hanging with us than hunting us. The dogs barked and lurched at her, but most of the time, their big white fluffy tails wagged in a friendly manner.

We were days away from heading out to Boston with Cate. I was a little uneasy leaving my eldest daughter Sarah to care for the dogs in light of our foxy friend. In thinking about how Sarah could handle the dogs in the event the fox closed in on her almost made me laugh. Here we were, about to see Cate undergo a very dangerous and serious surgery, and I was pontificating on how to handle a fox. A fox!

I had become just as twisted as this would-be pack member. I had actually begun looking for her and hoping to see her. It was becoming like one of those toxic relationships that should never happen, but the need to interact raged heavier than the logic to not.

The Threads of Messages

While we were in the midst of our final packing and preparations for Cate's surgery and our long week away, the fifth anniversary of my father's passing weighed on my heart. I no longer had that terrible pain that came when I thought of how he was no longer with us on this earth. Instead, there was an acceptance and a terrible, deep-rooted longing to see him. I missed seeing him on holidays, missed watching him figure out crossword puzzles, and missed hearing his opinions about how politically charged his country had become. It was hard not to be able to share with him and seek his guidance and strength in dealing with everything that was going on in my life. My mother had recently battled squamous cell cancer on her legs and had finished seven weeks of radiation treatments, I was no longer at my job, and Cate was ill.

I would have given anything just to be able to share all of that with him.

The morning of the date that marked his loss, I had plans to visit my mom and then sit in prayer at my dad's ashes and meditate. I was surprisingly calm and stoic. I got up and began the day as if it were any ordinary day. I ate an early breakfast with my husband and then cleared the table and rinsed the dishes.

Looking out into the everyday landscape of my backyard, a familiar figure emerged from the mist at the edge of the woods. The fox walked out of the buffer zone and crouched down over a piece of ground that had a thin layer of snow. She cocked her head back and forth in a slow, methodical motion, arched her back, leapt, and with exact precision pounced on the ground and dug. She repeated the motion two more times, the last providing her with a rodent. I watched her engulf the poor little thing in her mouth, drop it, and then flip it in the air. How cat-like, I thought! She then threw the mouse into the air one more time and opened her wide mouth to show razor-like teeth. She crunched down and swallowed.

I stood perfectly still, repulsed by what I saw, and yet unable to look away. I watched as she marched on her way until she reached our inverted canoe set upon two wooden sawhorses and nestled between my shed and the woods. She jumped up onto the hull and peered out over the horizon. Her thin, lithe body so athletically suited for hunting stood at the ready to pounce and devour. Her black stocking legs were so vibrant against the orange belly of our canoe. She sat and stared at me through the window.

I watched her and smiled. Even in her barbaric moments, I was so intrigued by her movements and her being. She heard something within the wooded area and leapt into the brush and disappeared. Her visitation filled me with a sense of wonder. Her mystical visit subconsciously eased my grief, providing lightness to the heaviness of the day.

I went to visit my mom. Together we shared memories and talked of my dad and his life. She missed him terribly, but it appeared the grief had relinquished its dark grip on our hearts and no longer created a barrier between earth and heaven. I went and sat in a chair near the urn that contained my Dad's ashes and prayed and visited with him for the first time in a long time. I told him how scared I was and how my heart hurt for Cate. I poured out my sadness and concern for the days ahead. I asked him to stand with me in the next few weeks and provide a sense of comfort and help from across the veil.

I touched the cold urn as if it was his hand and walked away. On the drive home I thought about how this "relationship" with my Dad had evolved into me believing he could still hear and help me. As I pulled my car out onto the main road, a car was exiting a parking lot and I slowed to let them out. I was deep in thought and amazed at how far I had come with my grief.

Where are you Dad? Are you near? Do you know what is happening to us? I felt this gut-wrenching pain from deep within my solar plexus and spewed it out into the open air with such intensity that I actually startled myself. Deep sobs emerged from inside me and I could not stop the roller coaster of emotions that soon seemed to take over my body.

Suddenly the SUV I had let out of the parking lot stopped to avoid something in the road and I became aware of their license plate. The license plate read "JUDE." I blinked and stared. I could not believe it. That was the name my father called me. Only a handful of people in my life can call me that and my Dad was number one. I smiled. Was it a sign?

As we reached the red light ahead, both of our vehicles slowed to a stop. At the stoplight, I grabbed my cell phone and snapped a picture of the heavenly license plate. I followed the SUV until I turned onto my street.

When I arrived home, I looked at my picture on my phone and caught another astonishing sign. The car had a car magnet with the letters DFCI...Dana Farber Cancer Institute. I could not help but feel a sense of peace in my heart. I was not afraid anymore. My Dad would be with us to let us know Cate would be okay. He knew our pain and he was on the job.

The Threads of Trust

The morning we were leaving for Boston, we took the dogs out for their early morning walk. We were trying so hard to stay within the boundaries of an ordinary day while feeling the weight of something so hard looming before us. Although we walked in a normal fashion, following the same routes and spots, neither of us spoke. It was like we were afraid that if either of us uttered even a single word, the other might just crack. The dogs completed their business and we headed home.

We were nearing the end of our walk, but there had been no fox in sight. I was uneasy about the trip, and felt burdened by the magnitude of what we were facing. I desperately looked for the fox. If she would only emerge from where she lived, it would somehow provide a salve for my heartache and give me something to help fight the battle ahead.

Within that pleading from deep inside came a rustle of noise to my left. And there she was, emerging from a neighbor's side yard. She trotted along at a steady pace, fully aware she was heading towards us. But as she approached the sidewalk, she suddenly stopped. My dogs leaped in the air snarling and barking. But that fox looked up at us and actually sat. She did not run or scurry away, snarl or bark. She just sat, back erect and eyes blinking, and then wrapped her thick, full tail around her body.

My dogs stopped barking and Craig and I stood still. Then she bowed her head down. I looked at my husband and he at me. Not sure what to do, I whispered, "Let's move on home."

We commanded the dogs to "go" and they continued on their walk in silence. All four of us walked past the bowing fox and onto the road that led to our driveway. I peered over my left shoulder and watched her cross the road in silence.

"What the hell was that?" I questioned.

"I don't know, Jude, but I swear she let us pass," Craig responded with astonishment in his voice.

"I can't believe she stopped and let us pass by her. She sat and bowed her head!" I said.

"I don't know what she is thinking, but I swear she is not afraid of the dogs," Craig added.

We continued our conversation as we entered into the house and unleashed the dogs.

"I have heard that foxes are very smart and know exactly how far they can go without getting caught or attacked. I read that a fox can actually run in front of a chained dog, knowing how far away they have to be so the dog can't get them. Maybe she knows that we won't let the dogs loose and that we are the alpha of the pack. That we control them both."

Craig nodded in agreement, "One thing is for sure, she definitely thinks she is part of our pack."

That was a turning point for me. I knew in that instance she was not stalking us, but rather co-existing with us. It was clear that she intuitively knew her limits and that the dogs were included in those limits. Somehow, she trusted us enough to know we would hold on to those dogs and not let them attack her and that we would not harm her. Within that revelation of that day, I knew I could trust her.

That was the day I named her. I chose her name after one of my favorite childhood story books, *The Tales of Reddy Fox* by Thornton W. Burgess. Reddy would be her name. Although Reddy in the story book had a sly personality, I found my Reddy to be more astute.

Somehow her appearance and display of reverence comforted me. To have this fox trust that we would not harm her and allow us to simply pass went against all logic. It was almost supernatural.

I felt at peace with our impending day and what was to follow. It almost made me feel like I had to trust in God for what was meant to be and give my heavy heart some peace. We had allowed the rusty-red thread to enter into the tapestry fold and meld. The weave was about to take hold and the picture would be fantastic.

The Threads of Encouragement

We arrived in Boston on February 11th and went straight to the hotel to get ready and plan out our next 24 hours. Boston was not foreign to us, but it was not home either. We decided not to venture too far and chose to eat in the hotel pub for ease. It was actually pretty good and Cate ate well, knowing she would be starting her fast shortly. Our dinner conversation consisted of small talk and bad jokes. Although we all dined with gusto, none of us really had an appetite.

I remember trying to force the food down my throat as if it were chalk and then made light small talk as if the next day was not a big deal. We returned back to the hotel room and decided to make it an early night. Cate appeared nervous but had succumbed to the fate and faith of her surgery and hope for remission. I remember feeling so sad that my daughter was facing something I could not help her with. We all read for a bit, then one by one, we shut off the lights and tried to sleep. The night seemed endless. I recall saying good night to her and wishing it was me who was going for the surgery in the morning.

That night was a mixture of weaves that prevented any of us from getting a good night's sleep. Thinking about the threads of that evening, even now while I type this, is surreal. I have always envisioned them in a multitude of colors and hefts. I believe that those 24 hours were designed with so many varied colors because of the seriousness of what we were all embarking on and the colors represented the many emotions that twisted and knotted within us.

We awoke at 5:00 AM on February 12th and showered and dressed. Our plan was that we would walk to the hospital in the morning, one block away for 6:00 AM check in. Her surgery would begin promptly at 7:30. The Threads of Acceptance had once again found their way into our tapestries, but it was mixed with threads of a fear of the unknown. That morning walk, cold and brisk, was the best thing we could have done. It gave us pause to consider the hope that would come out of this surgery and allowed us to burn off some of our excess nerves.

Cate was quiet and reserved the entire morning. We were told we would be able to go with her into pre-op before she was given an epidural and prepped for anesthesia.

We waited in the patient lounge for her to be called, but it was very crowded, and seats were at a premium. The receptionist suggested we wait in the small library room around the corner. That room was definitely more inviting and less clinical. We silently walked down the hall to the room and found a round table with comfy rolling chairs and settled in for a few minutes, perusing the book choices on the shelves around us.

"Catherine Cosby," called the pre-op nurse.

Cate stood, so small and thin, shoulders drooped and grabbed her purse. They directed her into a room to change into her hospital gown. Craig and I anxiously waited to join her in the pre-op room and once again sat down in at the library table and waited to be called.

When they called for us, Craig and I stood and quickly followed the nurse into a room filled with gurneys of patients preparing for surgery. Cate was in a corner chatting with her nursing team, confirming the information on her identification wristband. "Name, date of birth, allergies" were asked and confirmed at least 10 times by her pre-op nurse, doctor, anesthesiologist, and members of the hospital's administrative staff. All the buzzing and beeping of machinery and conversations made me dizzy.

Cate seemed, for the most part, calm, although understandably nervous.

The only melt down she had during the entire experience came when the surgical team did its final assessment and noticed she had not removed her daith piercing. The piercing of one of the inner folds of the cartilage in her ear had been done in the hopes it would help relieve her migraines. The opal stone that sat atop the piercing was a gift and try as we may, we could not get it to come out.

Cate began to lose her cool. She was so angry at the world and frustrated that when she finally got the earring to release, the gem flew off the loop and rolled under the top of the gurney. It was wedged between the base of the mattress and the bed frame and she began to unravel.

I rushed to reach it and accidently pushed it out of the frame and sent it rolling across the floor between other patient gurneys. It was like watching a slow-motion bit in a movie. Just as I got to where that little opal stopped, an orderly walked past and kicked into the opposite section of the room. Cate began to cry and lament that she wanted that opal found. Just then, the surgical team arrived to take her to the operating room. I tried my hardest to find that damn opal, but it had rolled into oblivion.

I turned around to see Craig kissing her on the forehead and I rose from my stooped position and ran over to follow her as they wheeled her toward the door. While they waited for the door to open, I bent down, kissed her and told her I loved her. I swear it felt like my heart would burst.

As they rolled her out of view I turned to Craig and cried, "That stupid opal!"

But it was pointless. We tried one more time to find it, but the pre-op was bustling with patients and we needed to move on. That crazy little moment had taken the edge away from standing and saying a formal goodbye. As disappointed as I knew Cate would be over the loss of the gift, there was a part of me that was grateful. It had been the perfect diversion to keep me from falling apart in front of her.

Five hours later we were greeting Cate in recovery and were working our way into a hell week of pain management and healing.

We entered into her recovery cubicle for just a few minutes to say hello, expecting to see Cate barely awake. What we saw instead was a locomotive of energy and determination. Cate was pumped full of pain killers and drugs and was hooked up to so many tubes and IV pumps that beeped and rang alarm bells that she looked like something out of the exorcist. Linda Blair would have been impressed.

She was awake when we entered and slightly elevated on a pillow. Her hair was untamed and messy and her eyes were dark and wild. Her pale skin, aside from the darkness that had settled around her eyes almost glowed.

She had become extremely irate because she was very thirsty and no one would give her water. She was not able to drink yet per post-operative rules—not even an ice cube—but she could have a sponge swab dipped in water to wet her lips. This outraged my tiny titan of a daughter. I half expected her to levitate above her mattress, speak in tongues, and drown us all in the water she was desiring. When they told us our fifteen minutes of visitation was over, I could not have been happier. I bestowed a blessing on the staff that would have to enter Cate's lair and breathed a sigh of relief knowing that her mighty personality was rearing its little head. It would take all the fight she had in her to get through recovery.

With a few room snafus taken care of, Cate was whisked away onto the fifteenth floor and was placed in a room with an incredible view of the Boston skyline. We settled in, ready to make this our temporary home away from home. With the surgery behind her, we had to face the long week of managing pain and getting her to heal.

Cate shared her room for a few days with a lovely young woman who appeared to be very ill. Her roommate was in her early 30s and although I do not know the reason for her hospitalization, I do believe she had cancer. I assumed this by her lack of hair and sallow complexion. She was a kind young woman with a nice smile and a sadness about her as she looked at Cate. I don't know if she assumed Cate was as sick as her, but I do know that she understood the constant blood draws and number counts.

I don't believe the young woman's prognosis was good, and on Cate's third morning in the hospital, the woman made a phone call to a friend and then proceeded to request that she be discharged from the hospital. The staff tried many times to discuss with her the gravity of her decision and how they were against her leaving the hospital care, but she had resolved that she had enough and wanted to go home.

As I listened to her voice and her matter-of-fact approach, this frail woman was incredibly formidable. The staff reluctantly agreed and went to draw up her discharge papers. They unhooked her IV and she dressed and began to pack her belongings. Her friend called her cell phone to let her know she had arrived. She seemed relieved.

"Great, thanks. See you in a few. By the way, could you grab two large strawberry and banana smoothies on your way up?" she asked with a lilt in her voice.

As she ended the call on her cell she stood up and put on a deep blue down coat, grabbed her bags, and waited.

My heart ached for her. We had met so many people through this ITP journey and a countless number of them, I am sure, are no longer here. I innately knew this was a life changing choice for her. She was choosing quality over quantity. She wanted to live her life on her terms.

The friend, a pretty woman with a very trendy coat arrived a few minutes later with her purse over her shoulder and a smoothie in each hand. They both smiled and embraced each other.

"Ready to go?" her friend asked softly.

"I am all set. Let's go home," the young woman said sweetly, signed the last of her paperwork, and stood.

Again, the medical staff had asked her to please reconsider or return if she felt unwell. They repeated the severity of her decision, but she was firm but kind.

She just shook her head and said, "I want to go home."

I had not really taken in how very thin she was until I saw her in street clothes, her delicate frame lost in her blue down coat. She was so pretty, with a girl-next-door kind of appearance. She was weak, but she walked with a defiant gate.

She grabbed the two smoothies from her friend and asked if she could grab the suitcase. She walked towards Cate with the sweetest of smiles and said, "Good luck with everything," and handed over one of the smoothies.

"I thought you might enjoy this."

Cate smiled for the first time that week and happily took the smoothie.

"Thank you!" she said gratefully.

And before I could offer to pay for it or say anything myself, the young woman left the room.

I think Cate was so wrapped into her own world of healing I don't think she understood the gravity of that moment. Her roommate was sharing something deeper than just a smoothie. She was sharing a pay-it forward moment with someone she knew was fighting just as hard as she was for good health and a chance. Somehow, she read Cate and knew that they fought the same inward battle with fierceness and tenacity. I was in awe of them both.

On the fourth day, Cate looked to be handling the pain well. She had an epidural block the first three days where she could press pain medication as needed. It worked beautifully for her and seemed to really help her turn a corner faster. On the fourth day, they removed it and slowly helped her to face the pain with minor pain meds. She was using a small pillow on her waist to help her sit and move more fluidly. Her hair had not been washed since the previous Sunday. I offered to brush it for her to which she happily and readily agreed.

I sat at the edge of the bed and began to gently brush the wisps of strawberry blonde hair around her face in light, straight strokes. She leaned forward, pressing her body on the small pillow for support to allow me to continue the process when a clump of hair came out from the back of her head and was entangled in the brush.

I stopped. Stared at her head, mortified. The only thing that held my shock in check was my fear of telling her I held a large tuft of her hair trapped in the brush. I looked to where I had brushed. There were multiple bald spots. I swallowed hard, afraid to tell my daughter her long, luxurious hair was falling out. She evidently became aware of my fumbling and hesitation to continue brushing her hair in full strokes.

"Cate...," I uttered.

She smiled and said, "Mom, it's okay. It has been falling out for weeks. It's the Nplate, it's normal."

"Why didn't you tell me?" I asked.

"Because you were already going through so much, I did not want to upset you with one more thing," she said quietly.

"Oh," I replied.

What could I say? Nothing.

What could I do? Nothing.

My daughter was losing her hair and there was nothing we could do.

I finished the brushing and handed her makeup bag over to her. I stood and put the brush back in her suitcase and looked out over the landscape of the city below. Behind me, I could hear her and Craig talking about something, but it could have easily been in the next room. He had no idea what had just happened. I just stared out at the city as the tears ran down my face.

I excused myself, mumbling something about needing to use the bathroom and stepped out into the hall. I went into the hospital wing bathroom and wept. Hard.

I chastised myself while standing in front of a bank of mirrors over the sink.

Don't be silly. It is just hair. It will grow back.

But I couldn't stop the tears from rolling down my face. My baby was sick. I kept telling myself it's not that bad.

But it was.

What I learned in those profound moments was that Cate was stronger and more resilient than I gave her credit for. She handled all the doctors, nurses, meds, and pain with such grace and composure. She was so young and yet so old. Cate had also begun to read me, I believe, and chose to protect me from some of the things that would break my heart. I knew that without this incredible bond we had forged, neither one of us would have walked this walk with such determination.

She had even taken the time to contact the Rehab Facility she was supposed to be working for and explained that her recovery was going to take even longer than she anticipated due to the surgical procedure and subsequent visits. Her immune system was compromised and that also presented limitations on her exposure to the public. Her dreams were receding, being carried further and further away from her by the tides of her disease, but her heart still held true to the idea that she would overcome it all and still be able to be a part of their team.

In the days to come, she did everything she was supposed to do and more. She took long strolls and did laps around the circular hallways of that 15th floor of Brigham and Women's like a pro. In those days, while I was fighting for some form of release in my gut, I watched with amazement as she set the tone for her recovery.

She joked continually with the staff, and we found that the staff gravitated to her room to tell funny stories and kid with her as well. They were intrigued by the singular cornrow braid in her hair and the homemade bead that was fastened to it. I threatened to cut it off while she slept and blame the surgeon. We had fun amid the pain and made a point to keep our unordinary life, as ordinary as possible.

I liked that. Even though our days were far from typical, if we strived to make and see them that way, maybe the universe would grant us this wish. Ordinary days embraced within ordinary moments.

I liked the thought of creating normalcy in our world with simple gestures and conversations. We celebrated Valentine's Day in the hospital with fun little gifts and tokens. I went down to the hospital gift store and bought Cate crazy pens, ocean-themed puzzle books, and goofy socks. Her boyfriend, Taylor, drove up to Boston with flowers and spent the day hanging out in her room.

Could we have "ordinary" on this road we were stuck on? Why, yes, we could! Craig and I snuck away with the nurses urging and recommendation of a lovely pub not far from the hospital. We walked several blocks down the road and had a romantic Valentine's Day supper surrounded by stringed lights and a beautifully lit bar. Craig surprised me with a beautiful heart necklace encased with beautiful gems that he had stowed away in our suitcase before we left for Boston.

I treasure that necklace for so many reasons. But mostly because it reminds me that within that setting of sadness and healing, we managed to create ordinary moments and make them special enough to shine within our tapestries.

The Threads of Perseverance

One week later, we said goodbye to Cate's hospital room and began our two-hour ride home with our patient, almost bubble wrapped, in the back seat of our Cadillac. She tolerated the moving car and bumping ride beautifully and we returned to our home in Western Massachusetts to a huge bouquet of flowers and balloons and well wishes. Cate was on her way to remission.

Shortly after Cate's initial diagnosis, I had begun journaling. It was, in some regards, a way to disclose my fears and inner feelings without sharing them out loud. It became a cathartic exercise for me, a place to find release.

It was in this writing that I was forced to come to the conclusion that Cate and I, if we were going to make it through, were going to have to walk this difficult path together. Multitasking had always come easily before Cate's illness, but after she was diagnosed, that all changed for me. I found that the illness and treatments were so exhausting, both mentally and physically, that I had little energy or willpower to focus my attention on anything else. Why this changed, I can't answer. I think that once we both recognized that the road was permanent, not just a temporary detour, I knew I had to mentally adjust to that.

During this recognition of my limitations, I was plagued with guilt. I rationalized that there were so many others who had it harder with much tougher battles to fight. Children who were actually terminal, or had passed, or fought more severe illnesses than Cate. This way of thinking would always bring me to a point where I felt I had no right to fall apart or be sad. Somewhere deep in my mind, I had convinced myself that my daughter's illness was somehow less and that I should just be stronger and more flexible in dealing with the challenging hand we had been dealt.

It was during those moments of lamenting, when her platelet count was stable and life appeared normal, that I felt the most embarrassed that I was so emotional about her infirmity. But then her platelets would crash, treatments would ensue, side effects would commence, insurance issues would arise, and I was forced again to deal with an overwhelming and horrible feeling of helplessness. I would look at her medical bills, totals of over $300,000 paid by the insurance company, and would begin to feel a queasiness in my gut. It wasn't the money, but rather the black and white visual of the severity of her health. The insurance company would never agree to pay that exorbitant amount of money for health care if it wasn't warranted.

My daughter was ill. Seriously ill.

Even now, just writing those words stings.

Analyzing this reflection of where I was at that point is when I found the most extraordinary revelation of my level of life. I had to first be able to accept this hardship without denying any other outcome. In being able to do so, I had to actually "see" that my daughter was sick. Whether she was sicker than most, but not as sick as others, had no bearing on what she was going through. Guilt had to be removed. I had to be true to how I felt and how hard this was for me and let others deal with their own views. Doing so helped me be more effective in how I was going to face the future with an adult child who might require my assistance well into her future. I had to also accept that this illness could affect the quality and quantity of her life and the plans she had for her future.

The second part of this acceptance was to actually see the truth before me. Not the wishful truth or the imagined truth, but the actual facts before me. To do so, I had to let my Acceptance Thread loosen and resew a section of my tapestry. I would have to use my Power Thread, my Revisiting Pain Thread, and the Thread of Overcoming to help me redesign this part of my tapestry so that I could smooth out the bumps and make a more defined hopeful picture.

Before the diagnosis of ITP, my daughter, Cate, was a confident, vivacious, energetic, athletic perfectionist. But in the two years since her diagnosis, Cate had morphed into another version of herself. Her confidence had waned completely from the lack of energy and the lull in her career goals. Her vivaciousness was met with more of a passive demeanor, her energetic self was constantly afflicted with fatigue from the illness and meds, and although she was still a perfectionist, her memory was affected by some of the meds and she required sticky notes and reminders to keep her on task.

But what saddened me most of all was that her frailty kept her from all the physical things she loved to do. Hula hooping was met with careful reservation because of bruising. Running was too much for her and walking long distances required intermittent rests to complete. Inability to do all the things she should be able to do in her early 20s had aged her mindset into that of a much older person. She was riddled with anxious tendencies due to what I referred to as the "Russian roulette" of weekly blood counts. She became a slave to those counts and what they meant for her. There was a level of foreboding when we could not figure out why her platelets continued to decline with the same previously effective treatments. Each time this happened, I could feel her growing hopelessness, almost like she was helpless to its will. She became fearful of social engagements when her immunities were too low. It was a crappy existence and my heart ached for her.

In the scope of really understanding why this had become so overwhelming to both of us, we became the dynamic duo. Every visit and decision was made as if we were one. I don't know, even at this point, if that was good or bad. I felt she was so overwhelmed that she needed to have someone help her navigate through the major decisions whether that be making treatment decisions or acting as a liaison when seeking insurance pre-authorizations. In agreeing to let me be her wingman, I worried that she would adopt the mindset that she needed someone to help her, that she was incapable of taking care of herself.

I needed to find a happy medium.

In accepting this whole grand picture into our tapestry, we were able together, to create a better road to work on and follow. I don't feel embarrassed or apologetic anymore, nor do I allow guilt to make me feel like I have to remain positive and cheerful at every turn. That does not mean I don't have a positive outlook or can't effectively handle this situation. What it means is that Cate and I are a team and we will continue to battle this disease and find a more productive and faithful way of living with it.

I believe that those who walk along with a loved one who suffers from physical or mental infirmities can identify with how easy it is to become bewildered and weak themselves. For me, journaling allowed me to see these unsure stitches and identify my shortcomings. This awareness helped me cling to my strengths to bolster the weave. When I realized that I was capable of walking the same path with different purposes, I was able to amass the strength and courage to finish the road and support both Cate and myself.

In a separate journal, I also started to write about my interactions with Reddy. Whereas my journal about Cate's journey was about putting my angst and frustrations on paper, journaling about the fox was more therapeutic. I was able to create a world that documented the experiences I was having as an observer, leaving the pain of my current life aside. The Threads of Perseverance had begun to stitch a fresh essence into my being and I had the opportunity to experience something totally unusual.

As we had unpacked the car on our return from Boston, I asked Sarah if there were any sightings of the fox.

She replied, "Nope, not at all."

I instantly felt sad, as if that little world I had become so used to had disappeared while we were away.

Busy with keeping Cate's pain regulated, Craig and I had set up a schedule for around-the-clock care for the next few days. Our objective was simple: to keep Cate as pain-free as possible. That meant we had to keep her on her pain meds at regular intervals, every two and a half hours, and change the lidocaine patches that kept her comfortable.

While standing at our kitchen counter and perusing the written schedule of meds, I suddenly had the urge to look out my window into my backyard. I had mentally prepared myself for the nights ahead and something within me longed for some form of comfort. Nightfall was beginning and darkening the outside landscape. I noticed something scurry along the back corner of the yard. My heart leaped for joy, for I knew that familiar shape! It was the fox! Reddy had come for a visit.

She moved a little stealthier than I was used to and seem scattered in her hunt among the bird feeders. I tried to get her attention, but she would not look at me. I followed her as she intently moved toward the back of my house and closer to my window. I assumed I would get a familiar reaction or look from the fox, but she seemed much more intent on finding food than on connecting with me. The fox looked up quickly, scanned a corner of the yard and suddenly scurried away in fright.

This fox's movement was a little more erratic than I was used to, but because of the darkening sky, it had become more difficult to see. I stretched my body so tight over that countertop that I could feel the muscles tightened in my calves.

The fox stopped near the wood line, standing up on her hind legs. Why would she do that? It was then I realized that she seemed larger than before, and her coloring was a deeper red. In the fading light I spotted a bright white tip to the tail and then I knew. This wasn't Reddy. It was another fox! Where was my little friend? Had something happened to her?

As the days went on and while Cate convalesced, I began to interact more with Reddy and her friend. I began to take pictures of her and the fox I decided was her mate. I named him Rodney.

Rodney was a classic fox. He was gorgeous but aloof and very protective. He had absolutely no interest in me or forming any kind of alliance with a human.

Reddy was different. Not just in her personality, but even in her physical makeup. Her coloring was dull in comparison to him, but though he wore a prettier coat, Reddy outshone him in one other significant way: her face. Her familiar face was capable of such expression. Her eyes were warm and soft and it often appeared as if she smiled. I would stare at her and feel like I knew her, and even more profound, as if she knew me.

❧

The Threads of the Winter had begun its weave of fresh starts and painful moments. It was a name I purposely gave to the thread and span of time that began as 2018 approached.

Each one of us has the capability to entitle each section of our tapestry with its own given name, as one would name a file or a title of a book. When we are approaching a new phase that may bring about a change in a path or a shift of events on the road we are currently traveling, naming it or identifying this stitch allows us to become more open to the possibility that our current picture is about to change in a very profound way.

Within the stitches that began to weave each segment of the Winter Thread, it became apparent that I was reaching out for some sort of solace and peace. The threads of ordinary times began to fill my being with desire. I did not fully understand what it was in my tapestry that I was yearning for, but I did recognize that there was a shift within me and to understand it I needed some kind of outside guidance.

Although most of us do not want to begin the New Year on a canvas of uncertainty, we all have the ability to recognize and welcome the stitches that can soften those hard times. We persevere through the difficult times and hope to find new ways and new connections to help us through. Welcoming new souls, embracing humorous moments, , and loving the ordinary times of our lives can create a depth within us we did not know existed. Appreciating the normalcy of life and recognizing the importance it plays in the baseline of our tapestry is a gift. These golden threads are woven in the most simplistic moment of or lives.

2

The Threads of the Spring Weave

"If we had no winter, the spring would not be so pleasant: If we did not sometimes taste of adversity, prosperity would not be so welcome."

~ *Anne Bradstreet*

The Threads of Renewal

It was the first few days of March. Winter had begun to release its grip and rain replaced the snow, making the grounds muddy and wet. Our morning walks had become a different drudgery. No pristine white to distract us from the bitter cold, just muddy and dank snow within the rawness of the early morning chill. I was longing for the days when the snow would completely melt away, the ground would smell like spring, and the morning air would be filled with the sounds of the returning birds. The days had become lighter and flashlights no longer a requirement, but the warm spring and summer still felt so far away.

Cate seemed to be doing really well one month into her life without her spleen. She was getting stronger every day and her platelet count had become so out of whack that instead of being so precariously low they were now too high. Her oncologist hematologist explained that it was normal for the body to adjust to the missing organ. More than often these were not real platelets, but rather damaged ones waiting to be cleansed from her system. We would not know for another few months if it had worked. All we could do was hold tight, get her counts done, and try to relax and think positive thoughts.

Although she was really moving along physically, I remember one morning feeling like her outlook was also making progress. She had on a pair of black yoga pants that looked loose on her little figure and a pretty flowered sweatshirt I had bought her. She had done her hair and put on makeup and I felt for the first time in a long time she was getting back into the swing of things. I feared a potential depression was on the horizon and felt that her return to a normal beauty routine was a great sign of brighter things to come.

I was very excited to share some fun news with her about a visitor to my birdfeeders. Both my daughters had nicknamed me "Snow White" because I loved animals and made them a big part of my day. I noticed several kinds of woodpeckers visiting my new suet feeders and could not wait to share the new additions with her. I do believe that both of my daughters placate me with these silly moments because they know how excited I get.

I told her all about the little hairy woodpecker that was frequenting one feeder in particular and brought her to the window to see him. She smiled and nodded her acknowledgement of him. As we walked away from the window still chatting about the little guy, we heard a terrible thud behind us. Something had hit against my atrium door with tremendous force and I had a terrible feeling I knew exactly what it was.

"NO!" I yelled and went running to the living room.

"Oh my God! I killed my woodpecker! I put the feeder too close to the house! Oh no!" I lamented.

Cate looked at me with a mix of sympathy and wariness. I knew my reaction was over the top, but I don't like anything hurt or harmed on my watch.

Cate tried to be the voice of reason and said, "It might have been nothing mom," as she followed me into the living room.

Peering out of the atrium door, I scanned the ground for any view of a dead or injured bird. I saw nothing at first and began to calm when in the corner of the deck half buried in a tuft of a snowdrift, I saw the woodpecker, out cold, wings spread wide.

I opened the door and saw its limp body.

"Cate! Get me a pair of gloves! We need to pick it up and make sure it is okay."

Cate, as always, did what she was told, but I saw the look of skepticism in her eyes.

Seconds later she brought me a pair of gloves from the hall closet. Of all the gloves I own, my daughter had decided I should handle this injured, possibly dead bird, with a pair of my dress burgundy gloves with rhinestones sewn down the sides. I peered at her for a moment to discuss the choice she made and then decided to keep my mouth shut. If the bird was going to meet its maker, I supposed it might as well go in style.

I slid my dress gloves on and proceeded to lift the limp body into my hand and was amazed at the size of the bird and its beak. It appeared to have broken its neck and was completely unaware it was being handled. As I wiped the ice crystals away from its eyes, I noticed the woodpecker began to blink. I smiled.

"Cate! He's blinking!"

She appeared to be a little more interested in what I was doing now and came over to help with the recovery process of our little feathered patient.

We brought the bird inside and I sat on my couch. Cate grabbed a hand towel and placed it over my lap. I still held the bird within my gloves and began to carefully stroke his head, neck, and the back of his body. The woodpecker allowed me to touch his wings and straighten him out. Although he was not moving at all, he continually blinked at us and looked around the room. About 30 minutes later, he began trying to stand but kept one leg crunched in a ball. I wasn't sure what to do next.

I placed the bird on top of the bath towel that was still on my lap and continually stroked him and took each wing and gently massaged and moved it. This little woodpecker seemed to not be in any pain, which was a huge relief to me. He was constantly cocking his head and moving it in an inquisitive fashion, but sincerely looked like he was enjoying the massage he was getting. It also seemed like this little guy was taking in my living room and what it really was like inside one of these human "nests." It was pretty posh and very warm.

I asked Cate to snap a picture of me holding the bird and petting it. As a joke, we sent Craig a text with a picture entitled "Mom's new pet, Woody."

Craig texted back immediately "Are you serious, Clark?" and sent an animated gif of Cousin Eddie from the movie *National Lampoon's Christmas Vacation*.

Cate texted back "Yes."

I think Craig needed to process what was going on and shortly thereafter Cate's phone buzzed with a text.

"Is that thing in the house? In our living room?" he questioned.

Cate texted once again. "Yup."

"Great," was his reply.

After about an hour of nursing the bird, it suddenly stood on both feet and began to flap its large wings. I became excited and yelled to Cate.

"He is okay. He can stand and flap his wings! He isn't going to die!" I was practically bursting with joy and pride.

Looking at this *I Love Lucy* moment, Cate pointed to the three cats on the staircase and the two Great Pyrenees in the kitchen.

"Um, Mom, what is your plan when that bird starts flying in the house?" she said sarcastically.

My gleeful expression suddenly became pained.

"Crap, I did not think that part out yet. Do you think he is ready to go out and fly?" I asked.

Cate's response was simple. "At this point, I don't think that matters. I think he needs to go outside, NOW!"

I had to agree. There was no way I could save it from the beasts within my house, so I stood and walked towards the door out into the freezing cold, with no coat on but still wearing my pair of really kick-ass, glamourous gloves, the hairy woodpecker still in hand.

I opened the door to the deck and was immediately met with a blast of icy cold air. My long-sleeved t-shirt did little to shield my body from the 40-degree wind. I missed my warm living room. I do believe my feathered friend felt the same.

But I would not let a little cold air deter me. I stood victorious in my moment. In my mind, my little woodpecker friend was about to spread his wings and take to flight. I raised my arm to the sky, ready to bid him a fond farewell as he regained the sky and then...

Nothing.

He just sat there, nary a feather wag or wing spread to demonstrate a willingness to go.

I tried several times to encourage him with a flick of my arm.

Still nothing.

In fact, the woodpecker clung so tightly onto my hand that I could feel its little talons sticking through my gloves and into my flesh. I walked over to the bird feeder and tried to peel its little feet off of my finger and onto the mesh wiring of the stand.

Nothing.

Cate had followed me outside, snapping a few pictures of me in my laughable moments of glory, but it was freezing and I sent her back into the warmth of our house. I remained outside, freezing, with a bird refusing to release from my finger.

I peeled one bird foot onto the birdfeeder and did the same to the second foot. The bird immediately jumped back on my hand. This dance went on for a total of 20 minutes. I was beside myself. Teeth chattering and almost ready to let him have his way and join our rag-tag crew of species inside the house. In a final effort, I walked away from the bird feeder and over near my red bud tree.

I pleaded with my little stowaway. "It is time to go little fella."

And with that, it lifted off my fingers and flew into the tree. I stood astonished by the site. It took flight, and dove, whizzing by my head before flapping up onto a higher tree.

I smiled.

Walking back towards my deck, that little woodpecker swooped down once again and landed on a barren magnolia squawking at me.

"You're welcome," I exclaimed and off it flew into the woods.

The last of winter was melting away and despite the moments of despair and loss I had been feeling less than an hour before, I was feeling a sense of renewal.

The Threads of Rain

The first day of spring arrived with a cleansing light rain and I immediately felt the shift of the season. My walk with the dogs that morning was so pleasant and there was a true sense of "spring in the air." I hadn't seen Reddy for over three weeks, but on occasion, I would see the other fox, her mate, Rodney.

Rodney remained the classic fox, aloof and shy. His intense eyes and dark stocking legs would stand out against the dreariness of the backyard, but he was strictly there to do business. He viewed my yard as a hunting ground for small prey and leftover seeds. I would spy him occasionally sipping water that pooled in the bowl of our fire pit but other than that his visits were quick and efficient.

When I finally saw Reddy again, she was running in the rain, in an agitated state. She sprinted throughout the abutting yards in a fast and erratic manner for more than 20 minutes. I felt sorry for her because her little body was so drenched and it was a chilly rain. I was actually concerned that she was rabid because it was late morning, a time where we rarely saw either fox.

I happened to mention my concern over our neighborhood vixen, to a neighbor who knew I was fascinated by these creatures. She shared with me that they had recently seen a female fox living under their shed and that she had a litter of four light-colored kits. I was beyond excited! Maybe that is why Reddy was missing and Rodney was in my yard more frequently scavenging.

Could it be that she was a mother? How exciting it would be to be able to observe them as they grow! I had suddenly become interested in obtaining information on red fox kit development and had a multitude of questions about them. The more I became informed the more I became dismayed. The statistical facts were not in their favor, as many of the kits, or pups, can fall prey to predators like coyotes and bobcats. Some sites disclosed how at approximately four weeks of age they will begin to venture outside the den but still remain very close to home. They will begin to molt and their fur will begin to take on a reddish color. At about 12 weeks old they will leave the den and wander about to follow the adults and learn to forage for themselves. It is at this unfortunate time of their lives that many will not survive because they become victims to predators.

My heart sank.

My poor Reddy.

I made a vow that I would help her as much as I could.

It struck me as odd how involved I had gotten in the world of this little fox and how my energies clearly needed to focus on things closer to home. Yet in these moments, the break and distraction provided a much needed respite. It was as if I could leave my world behind and immerse myself into another realm.

This Rainy Day thread had both dampened and brightened my day. In turn, being able to witness my daughter's increasing strength also brought a lightness to my being that I had not felt in quite some time. These two melded together with a picture of newness and hope. It was erasing the cold and fatigue that the hard winter days had brought and issued a fresh and vibrant rebirth of life. I was feeling renewed and joyful.

The Threads of Rain are sent in waves that seem to dampen the world. But what I gleaned from this thread was a chance to wash away all the things that hardened and stuck to my tapestry, ushering in a sense of renewal to my soul and a brighter essence to my life.

The Threads of Catharsis

The end of April saw a healthier Cate and a more relaxed Judy. Cate had a very successful six-week check-up with her surgeon at Brigham and Women's. Her incision was healing beautifully, her platelet count was very high, but expected, and her energy level was returning.

At the time, I was still unemployed, a decision Craig and I had made so that I could focus on taking care of Cate and handle all the medical affairs like billing and insurance. It was an unusual time for me, but looking back I viewed it as a gift. I was able to concentrate completely on our home and devote myself entirely to getting her to all her appointments. I was her advocate and her personal assistant.

Cate, at her tender age, had relinquished all of her medical care into my hands and together we mapped out her treatments. She was extremely comfortable with having me in charge and there was nothing I did not know about her medically. There was no need for hang ups or embarrassment. Life was precarious and too unstable to care about personal issues.

With the positive feedback from her doctor, I decided we should take a day trip to our happy place—Newport, Rhode Island—and walk the bird preserve and the beach and just decompress for a short while. Cate was so excited with the prospect of spending a day near the ocean and allowing its mystical healing powers to envelop our bodies and soothe our minds. I told her all about Sachuest Point Natural Wildlife Refuge and the Island Rocks section of this magical place. This preserve would be our first stop.

We mapped out a plan to take the hike into the preserve. This beautiful shore is lined by thousands of rocks, rounded and smoothed by the breaking surf. I shared that this was the place where I had chosen the flat rocks to display in our rock garden in a namaste formation.

We decided to add a few more to our collection and just hang by the breaking shore. I promised her we would walk the beach and then dine at our favorite restaurant, the Brick Alley Pub, where we would share our favorite: the loaded nachos. I saw such an excitement in her demeanor that I could hardly wait to go.

We left early on a Thursday morning in late April and made our way into Newport in record time. As we crossed the great Pell Bridge, with its heavenly archways and the view of the Atlantic Ocean spanning the horizon, I swear we could hear our breathing change. Our inhales and exhales were more on target and our bodies vibrated with life. Every single time we cross that bridge it is always the same. It never gets old. I had shared once that I never want to take for granted the peace, serenity, and awe given to us by the crossing of the Pell Bridge. We both beamed and looked at each other.

"Here we are, Cate! Our beautiful beach awaits us," I exclaimed with joy.

She smiled, tight lipped, and leaned her head against the inside car window. The coolness of its touch to her forehead made her breathing easier. "Yes," she said with a long exhale.

We cruised into town and drove onto America's Cup Boulevard and passed by Bowen's Wharf. What was the magic of this place that seemed to alleviate the anxiety and tension within our tired bodies? Its mystical energy was evident, and we cruised up Memorial Boulevard and by the entrance of the Cliff Walk with anticipation in our hearts.

The view, as we descended the incline, was the breaking surf spanning across the shoreline of Easton's Beach. I looked over at her and she was just still. I knew in that instant we were about to step firmly onto the path to healing and I could not wait to show her my new discovery.

We continued on past Easton Beach, followed the one-mile drive past Purgatory Chasm, and then drove along the windy road past the stretch of beach that spanned the horizon.

We drove toward our planned destination taking in the sights along the way. We passed Surfer's End and admired the small group of surfers lulling in the choppy surf. We meandered a bit and continued onward past Second Beach and onto the windy road to the preserve. We passed through the entrance of Sachuest Point. An American flag waved proudly in the gusty wind. Large tufts of seagrasses billowed along the road and we rolled down our windows to let the salty air fill the car.

Our anticipation was palpable as we chatted about sunblock, ways to carry our treasures home, and how beautiful the weather was for this adventure.

As we neared the preserve entrance, the starting point for our rock-gathering adventure, I was forced to a stop by a blockade set across the road.

A large orange sign read: Closed for Construction.

How was it even possible that on the only day of the year that we decided to drive two hours to visit this little mecca, it would be closed to allow for the construction of a series of speed humps?

I instantly felt like Clark Griswold in *National Lampoon's Vacation* when he drives all that way through all kinds of adventures to find that Walley World was closed! I went into a tirade about how unfair this was. Why would they have to close for something so stupid?

All I could do was shake my head in disbelief. It wasn't fair.

Cate could not hide her disappointment and I felt anger surging up inside me. How could the universe be so cruel? To let us anticipate this day with such joy only to rip it away from us.

The nearest area to park was a good mile down the road and too far for Cate to walk, especially when we would already have a long walk to conquer to get to the island rock area.

"What do you want to do?" I questioned with a sigh.

"It's up to you Mom. I'll do what you want us to do," Cate said, trying not to sound too disappointed.

"How about a walk on the beach and some shell collecting? Then we can go into town, eat, shop, and head over to the Cliff Walk for a short walk and look for sea glass?"

"Sounds good," she replied.

I tried to read her, but she was so guarded about showing her disappointment. I instantly became hell-bent on turning this all around. We were going to make our day special somehow. I had to remain open-minded. This was a small disappointment to bear in comparison to all the other things we had been through. I had this.

We rounded the corner of the blockade and headed back down about a mile to the beach entrance and its ample parking lot. As we stepped outside into the sunshine and fresh air, we could hear the roar of the waves crashing into the shore. Inhaling the fresh, salty air and closing my eyes to the sun on my face, I immediately felt the boom of the surf enter my entire body.

Serenity.

The rest of our day was perfect and I began to understand the reason for our disappointment. We had come to this place for solace, not for a quest of island rocks and namaste. We had been given this blessing in late April for so many reasons. I was not working at this time, so freedom to spend a day like this was guilt-free and without reservation. Cate was healthy enough to not only make the trip, but enjoy the day. The fact that our quest was redirected was not a big deal.

Cate and I walked along Second Beach and let the chilly spring water envelop our feet and swirl sand between our toes. It was something that an April day a year ago would never have allowed. We talked deeply, emotionally, and freely about all that had plagued us both in the past 14 months. It was as if each rush of the water and each ebb of the waves released pain from our hearts and allowed us a new-found freedom, a catharsis to our weary souls.

During this time of her recovery, Cate and I established a silent partnership. In spending a day like this in our favorite spot, we allowed peace and tranquility back into our lives. We had given ourselves this day to reestablish a balance of our everyday lives with our spiritual beings. Within this mecca of sea and sand, we rejoiced in the simplicity of the moments. It was medicine for our mind, body, and soul. We learned so much about ourselves that day. Our conversations led us to be open to our dark places and our pain, as well as our hopes and future goals.

We sat by the water's edge using our sweatshirts as a blanket to sit on and allowed the wind to blow our hair and the sun to kiss our faces. The sand still held onto the coolness of the spring air and did not warm at all in the sun. It chilled us a bit and I asked if she was ready to move on to other things.

"Ready, Freddy?" I asked.

"Just a sec," Cate said and fumbled in her purse for something.

Grabbing her cell phone, she snapped a selfie of us on that beach, the Atlantic Ocean as our backdrop and the Wildlife Refuge in the far distance. My thick, curly hair made a blanket of swirls around my face and her long, strawberry blonde hair, now getting fuller with each day, flew in the wind. What a glorious picture of us! It is one of my favorite memories of that day.

I still look at that picture and feel thankful that such a beautiful image was embroidered into my tapestry. It captured the essence of that day. Stitched within that snapshot and other pictures from our trip are a variety of threads: clarity, mindfulness, beauty, love, and most of all, acceptance. Those intricate threads had been placed before us to weave this glorious picture of our special day.

Namaste in a different form: the gift of an ordinary day.

The Threads of Sweet Remembrances

With April closing out and the summer in the near distance, my mood started to lighten. I was getting back into the rhythm of life. In the midst of my adventures with Cate and her slow but steady recovery after her splenectomy, my mom and I would get together or phone each other every day and chat. She shared her wisdom through humor and hindsight. Our conversations were simple and sweet. We loved to tell each other the best deals of the day for our grocery lists, the latest inconvenient detour for road work, and the crazy politics of the day. We also discussed Cate, Sarah, and my mom's own battle with skin cancer.

And she absolutely loved to hear about Reddy.

She would listen to the stories of my little fox friend and crew, delighted in the stories of their antics of the day. These light-hearted conversations with my mom kept me grounded and reminded me what life really was all about.

Mom was recovering from squamous cell skin cancer on her legs and I had been her ride for seven weeks of daily radiation in the fall of 2017. In April 2018, she was still healing from the ravages of lengthy radiation treatment. Her legs were in constant pain and she had severe burns on her left leg. My sisters and I had a regiment of making sure all her needs were met and that she was kept well fed and cared for. For me, that included talking with her over the phone every morning.

Mom had become more retrospect in her thinking and had wanted to share many of the childhood experiences she had while growing up in Fall River, Massachusetts during the Great Depression.

I am not sure if it was so that these memories would be kept alive and perpetuated through generations or if she intended to give me a life lesson within those gems of wisdom. Whatever the reason, I was open to listening and made a point to remember the impact of each story.

On this particular day in late April, we were discussing the bravery of our World War I and World War II veterans, especially those who fought on the beaches of Normandy. Mom was very passionate about the young soldiers who had given their lives in service to their country and those she knew and remembered.

She told me how, to my grandmother's dismay, my Uncle Dave had enlisted in the Navy on his 17th birthday to go and fight in World War II on the USS Guam. My grandmother ordered a beautiful red, white and blue birthday cake to celebrate his birthday and departure. They were a poor Irish family in the mill town of Fall River and there were not many bakeries back in that day. It was a luxury to have a cake, but my grandmother wanted him to leave with a special party. All four siblings and my grandmother were waiting for him to come home and placed the cake and plates on the table. My mother, 10 years old at the time, could not wait to eat that cake. They waited for him to walk through the door with such anticipation for the celebration that was to commence.

As my Uncle Dave walked through the door and was met with his mother and siblings, he smiled. He was ready for the adventure that awaited him. My grandmother was very emotional and had a hard time watching her eldest son leave for the ravages and dangers of war.

"We all sat down to serve the cake and wish my brother *bon voyage*, but suddenly no one wanted to cut the cake or eat it. We all realized what it meant. My brother was leaving. Not just leaving Fall

River, but leaving the country to fight in a war. The meaning and the weight of his enlistment had not fully hit us until that moment."

"Even my brother did not take a piece of cake," Mom said.

She shared that not one of them ever ate a single bit of that cake. It sat for days, uneaten. It represented the sadness of one of their own leaving and possibly for good. Luckily, my uncle did come home from the war. But there were so many who did not.

This story struck me so hard because it represented the trials of every family, no matter the issue. I could imagine what my grandmother went through, and it felt, in some way, familiar. We both understood the feeling of anxiety over the unknown present in the face of something bad or harmful that we have no control over. I suddenly felt a kinship to my grandmother and her plight. She never left for war, never engaged in the fighting, but a piece of her heart and soul stood on the front lines in the form of her son.

In listening to these stories, I began to recognize how life unfolds for all of us. As we progress on our given paths, it is so important to hold our past close to our hearts. Not just our own past, but that of our family. Hearing how past generations lived, labored, and lost was an important part of what I was currently facing. Life was going by and I needed some sense of clarity, something to keep it all in perspective. Within the strands of this life lesson on family hardship, we had another conversation about the impact that some decisions can have on the entire family unit. We discovered through this discussion that although a family can be steeped in love and respect, certain events or situations can have a rippling effect, for good or for bad, on the entire group. Hardships can bring a family together, and it can tear them apart. This discussion had a profound impact on me and I took that statement to heart. I promised myself that I would do everything in my power not to let the stress and difficulties of this road we were on tear my own family apart.

She stopped mid-sentence and said, "There are plenty of negative things we can remember about the people in our lives, but there is so much good to remember as well."

Within that simple statement was another pearl of wisdom. We can all get hung up on the negative of life and how people hurt or alienate us, but the truth is that life is a flash in the pan and to waste that kind of energy on the negative steals our happiness. I had recently started walking that darker path. I'd spent too much time focusing on the negative and that sentence pulled my Threads of Clarity and Mindfulness with a great tug and redirected me onto a better path.

"You know Mom, that is so true. From now on, I choose to remember all the good things each person has given me, rather than the bad. It already makes me feel better," I said.

"Me too," she replied.

We laughed a bit, but something in my demeanor must have faltered.

"What's wrong?" Mom asked, a worried tone in her voice. "You sound different."

"Nothing, really," I replied. "I am just really tired. Exhausted physically and mentally. I have this weird cough at night that keeps me up. I think I am coming down with something."

"Well, you need to go and rest. Leave everything for another day. There is only one you. Take care of yourself." She continued, "You are the classic case of the sandwich generation with major care on two ends. You have your family of course, but you have me at one end and Cate at the other. Both with high-level needs. It can be overwhelming. Take some time for yourself and I will check on you tomorrow."

"Thanks, Mom, you're right. I'm going to chill and Netflix something," I replied.

We laughed and said our goodbyes.

About an hour later my cell phone vibrated. I opened the text and a smile immediately came across my face.

"This is the piece of bread on the opposite side of Cate's piece of bread. How is our filling feeling?"

Life was constantly reminding me that the treasure of a normal day was a true blessing.

The Threads of Grace

As May approached, Cate was getting stronger. At her eight-week post-op visit, the surgeon commented that Cate was healing nicely. She was right on target with becoming an ITP success story. We were certain she was among the 70 percent of patients who saw success after a splenectomy. Her three-month check at Dana Farber was nothing but good news and her oncologist hematologist was very pleased with her prognosis.

And then we were given the best news of all—no maintenance meds, no weekly blood draws, only a monthly check with a platelet count blood draw would be necessary. Cate could have a normal life! We celebrated by going to the healing garden on the third floor of Dana Farber.

When the elevator doors opened to the third floor, we exited in perfect motion. We were one unit of sheer joy and hope. Craig pulled the large glass doors that led to the healing garden and held them open as we quietly entered the room. It was late in the day and there were no other visitors in the garden. The heady aroma of hydrangeas, orchids, and other vegetation greeted us the minute we stepped inside. The sounds of water and the kinetic art installations spun above us was so invigorating.

The healing garden is a mecca of plants and water features that make you feel like you've entered a hallowed ground of spiritual hope and belief. I was always drawn to that place, and Cate and I spent time there on many of her visits. This time we took pictures of her. It almost felt like a graduation of sorts and we relished the moments in that room. It was so empowering. Pictures with her parents, pictures with her boyfriend, Taylor, and pictures alone. All were representative of the journey we had shared with her and the success we all felt. It was as if we were saying good-bye to this place with a gratefulness that was never felt before.

We exited Dana Farber with a sense of grace, a mantra filled with grateful and thankful words for her blessing of health in our hearts. God had given her this gift and we completely planned on appreciating it.

Cate didn't want to tell too many people just yet. She had developed a slight paranoia of sharing good news only to have the floor drop from under her feet. I said I understood, but truthfully I did not. I wanted to scream it out to everyone. But I was not the one who had to go through all the procedures and treatments. It was not my body that had to face that disappointment, so I agreed and told only our closest family and friends.

We would wait to tell the whole world for a bit, just in case.

I truly believe in the opportunity to experience a level of Divine Grace. That day felt as if we had emerged from something so powerful and so profound. We were inspired to be there and to give thanks and accept the trial that had been bestowed upon Cate. Although none of us wanted or really understood why we were all faced with this difficulty, the grace we experienced that afternoon was so inspiring. Yes, Cate faced the physical trials of illness on how it impacted her body and her lifestyle, but we also faced the pain of watching her go through a difficult time.

What I had learned from our joined experience was that there is a fine balance between faith and trust. In order for this balance and harmony to remain in our life, we all have to put our complete faith in what we've been given and trust that no matter how the tides turn in the future, our family would be ok and that God would be there with us.

The Threads of Parenthood

We arrived home two and a half hours later, still high on life from the good news of Cate's good health, and tired. That night, from the front steps, I watched the goings-on across the street. Reddy, Rodney, and the four little, light grey kits played together among the great pines of my neighbor's back yard.

How I envied my neighbor! I secretly wished it was in my yard. If it was, I would sit on that back deck all day and night and never get a stitch of work done if only to watch their antics. I took video, pictures, and notes regarding them.

I began to relish this little family and decided it would be fun to journal their little lives, to watch them grow and interact with each other. Little did I know that in making that decision, I was leading my heart to witness so many heartbreaking moments. Or that ultimately, watching this family of foxes would lead me to discover much more about myself than I had ever imagined.

I began to really take notice of all their little personalities. The kits were born late March early April, so I guessed they were around seven weeks old. There was a big chubby one with an adventurous personality. I named him Perseus from Greek mythology because of his brave little nature. He stood out the most because he gave Rodney and Reddy a run for their money! They would corral the four kits and order them to return to their den under the shed. How they did this I did not know exactly. Could it have been a look, a soft sound, or a body movement? I never was able to figure it out, but whatever it was, Reddy or Rodney had it down pat and off the four would go, toddling and bouncing towards the shed. All four would wriggle their bellies and follow the dirt entry that led to their den.

No sooner were all four hidden from view, then out the opposite side would burst Perseus! He'd run straight for the back of the yard among the pine trees. This would infuriate his father, Rodney, who would become very forceful with his hell-raiser kit and physically force him back into the den. I could see by her body language that this made Reddy anxious, but I could not help but laugh at Perseus' roly-poly little body.

I did, however, realize that in disobeying his parents, he was also jeopardizing his safety as well as the pack's. Coyotes frequented our area, as well as a bobcat. It could prove deadly if he maintained his rebel ways.

Then there were Star and Moon. They were very similar in shade than the other siblings to me and they were inseparable. They did everything together. They sat together, exited the den together, and rarely played with Perseus or the other kit. It was a rarity to see them apart and it always made me feel sad to think that their closeness would end in just a short few months when they adopted the solitary lifestyle of an adult fox.

Then there was the runt. She appeared to be a girl to me and was just adorable. She was the lightest in color and presented as frailer than her siblings. This little fox never wanted to leave her mother's side, so it was hard to get her personality. In trying to name her, I thought it was best to give her something simple. She resembled Reddy the most and shadowed her wherever she went. She reminded me of Reddy's mini-me so I named her Reddy Girl.

From the majority of my observations I made over those next several weeks, Reddy Girl was one I guessed would not make it on her own. Rodney and the other kits had no real need for her. Reddy would tolerate her, but even she had begun to lose patience with this little fox and her needy ways. Reddy Girl nursed the longest and would rarely try to hunt live prey. She was always alone when Reddy was not near the den and I developed a soft spot in my heart for her.

This little munchkin continually tugged at my heart strings and I was hooked. With her goofy little movements and scrawny body, I could not help but feel protective of her. The pictures I took captured the story of her life. The others were strong and resilient, but Reddy Girl seemed nervous, uncertain, and afraid to venture too far from the den.

In truth, the way the kits learned to hunt was so cruel to me. I had to lecture myself on the ways of the natural world and what it took to survive in it. It was in watching these hard lessons that it became apparent to me that she was destined to fail and why she was so many times rejected by her siblings. She didn't mesh with the others and often did not seem to grasp the concept of hunting.

The parents would catch small prey, like a squirrel, mouse, or chipmunk. Then they would injure it enough to prevent it from getting away, but not kill it. They would bring it to the den and allow the kits to attack and kill it. It was barbaric to me, but it was in their nature and necessary for the young ones to learn to hunt, kill, and eat.

But Reddy Girl would not hunt, or if she did, not very well and instead preferred her mother's underbelly. If I had to guess, Reddy's natural side would have pushed the little one into a more active role of survival, but I sensed that she also knew this one needed more.

I had become almost obsessed with this furry family. Watching them. Protecting them. I began to talk with the neighbors about the foxes and assumed they would either think I was crazy or be reluctant to embrace them into our little community. What I found was the exact opposite. We all were secretly following them, protecting them, and yes, feeding them at times. They were, by some unique bit of fortune, like one of our own, and we meant to keep them safe.

The next few nights were rough. I had heard the coyotes in the distant farmer's field howling and yipping. Some nights it was unbearable. The lone howl, the repeat howls, then that frenzied, almost supernatural yapping of the entire pack. It was at the pinnacle of that horrible noise that all those who listened understood the hunt was closing in. Then almost as soon as it started, it would suddenly stop.

An un-earthly silence. It meant they had killed their prey.

I hated that silence.

Worse yet, it appeared to be getting closer each night. Our little fox friends were in peril.

Immersing myself into their little world and becoming an observer helped me to escape a little of my own heartache and gave me peace and enjoyment I had not experienced in a quite a while. I began to follow Reddy more intently and found her doing the same with me.

I would make a clicking sound with my tongue and she would come within moments. Sometimes, I would leave left over rolls of King Hawaiian Bread on a rock under my bird feeders. She loved those rolls and would devour them immediately and then graze around for seeds.

Reddy began to leave the den to hunt more and feed, but would ultimately return to the kits around midnight. I would sit in my bedroom on the second floor of our house and look across the road into the neighbor's yard. I felt like a voyeur at times, but it gave me the best view of their habitat. Inevitably, my neighbor's back light sensor would click on and in the dim yellow light, I would see the shadows of four little furry bodies running about the yard. It was so fun to watch. It was as if the ghouls of the night arose from their graves and danced about in a frenzied form on earth for a short while. Then, from somewhere within the thick pines that rimmed their property, the clear sound of a hoarse bark from one of their parents would emanate through the night air and within seconds the four would scramble back to their den. That led me to believe danger was not far and I prayed that they would remain safe.

The nights became a nerve wracking existence for me. In the middle of the night, I would get up and look out toward my neighbor's yard, as if my sentinel watch would keep anything from harming my little family. In the early dawn light, I was relieved to see their little bodies stretching and running about with mom and dad in the distance.

I made a habit of getting up at dawn and sneaking out of the house to check on them. I would tip toe, barefoot, silently over stones and sticks to get a closer look and hopefully get a picture!

Rodney did not like me to get too close. He would stare at me and be on constant guard. No matter how many times I had the chance to be around him, he never got comfortable with me. I respected his stance and inwardly knew he was not to be messed with. On the days when I pressed his tolerance, he would walk towards me in a fierce stance. I never failed to heed his message and would return to the middle of the road and watch from a distance. It was then that he would relax, sit, and look away, but always kept me in his periphery.

Reddy, however, was always open to me, and at times, I swear she liked my keen observation of them. Her daughter, Reddy Girl, also seemed at ease with me. I believe it was her deep connection to her mom that enabled her to witness the comfortable nature between Reddy and me. It was that bond that ultimately taught Reddy Girl to trust me.

Early on, I recognized that this little peanut let me take pictures much easier than the others. That was fun because I was able to really capture her silly spirit. When reviewing the pictures as time went on, I noticed Reddy Girl's right ear drooped. Not a lot, but enough that one could notice. I liked that about her. Her own little nonconformity that set her apart and made her unique.

The Threads of Innocence

The evening of May 17th was a hard night to handle. For two nights prior, the coyotes' howls had grown closer and closer. I could tell they were closing in around our neighborhood. The yipping started earlier than normal and by 10:00 PM their rapid howls were in full force. That entire night I could see the sensor light from my neighbor's backyard go off and on. Around 3:00 AM I was awoken by a terrible commotion of yapping from the coyotes and that terrible, hoarse, fox-warning howl. I slipped out of bed, looked across the street at the lights in the back yard and ran downstairs. I grabbed my car keys and ran outside to my car. Without even a sense of thought for myself, I slipped out into the night, barefoot, keys in hand and got inside my car. I sat in the driveway and continued to turn my car locks on and off and flash my car lights until the horrible ruckus stopped. I just knew my fox family was under attack.

Once it was finally over and the back light sensor no longer flickered on and off and the sounds had diminished, I had a serious moment of self-awareness.

What the hell was I doing in the car in the middle of the night flicking my lights on and sounding the car locks? Maybe I was losing it. How would one who has hit rock bottom know for sure? I remained still and looked out of the car window at the sky lightening in color. The car clock flashed 4:00 AM. Dawn would be coming in an hour.

"What the hell is wrong with you?" I whispered out loud looking into the rearview mirror at myself. My dark circles were ever present and my hair was a curly mess.

"Seriously?!?" I said, chastising myself and leaning my head back onto the headrest, momentarily closing my eyes in hopes that my rapid heartbeat would calm. I tried to use a controlled breathing technique to quell the anxiety attack I felt was threatening to erupt.

It was like I was losing my mind. It scared me. Loving animals and getting attached was normal for me, but this was different. I was sitting in the lonely night feeling this deep wound in my chest that would not go away. Why was I so intent on saving this little fox family? What was it about Reddy and her pleading eyes and her little kits? What was it about that little frail fox with the bent ear and scrawny tail? I stayed in the car awhile longer, just long enough to watch the pink of the sky light above the horizon. Then I went back inside and snuck back into bed. I was embarrassed and exhausted.

Something was definitely wrong.

Later that morning when I got up, I went to check on the kits. I immediately saw Reddy and counted...one, two, three... I scanned and scanned. I clearly saw Moon and Star closely huddled together by the side of the shed and Reddy Girl trailing tight to her mother's heels.

But where was Perseus?

I knew something had happened based on the terrible noises coming from the foxes and whatever had been on the attack. Reddy looked anxious and Rodney stood in alarm mode among the small forest of great pines that filled the property. My heart ached. Where was the bold and chubby Perseus?

At some point that day it became apparent that Reddy had moved her family and left their den. My neighbor with the shed that had sheltered our neighborhood fox family confirmed they had moved on. He had gone and looked under his shed but the only trace that remained were two squirrel carcasses and a few random bones.

That night proved just as loud and torturous. I spent the entire night staring out into the darkness trying to protect my little fox family with a litany of prayers and thoughts. Anyone who knew me would have thought I had lost my marbles. Damn, even I thought I had. What the hell was this? I was an adult woman with a sick daughter. I had recently left my long time job to take on the burden of this illness and here I was spending my valuable sleeping time protecting a bunch of foxes.

The following morning, I got up early to watch the long-awaited royal wedding of Megan Markel to Prince Harry. I wanted to watch the beautiful pomp and circumstance and see her gown. At 8:00 AM my cell phone buzzed with a text message from my neighbor, Rachel, across the street. Rachel knew my heartache and shared a bit of good news with me.

"We have the fox family living under our shed. Would you like to come by and see them?" it read.

My only response was "Yes!!!" and off I went to get dressed. *What wedding?* I mused!

I put on my flip flops and ran across the street and into their front door. Once inside, their daughter, Emily, brought me over to their back window and there I watched and videoed on my cell phone the three little kits play. I could not believe it! How wonderful. The little one, Reddy Girl, ran away and under a bush the second we all walked outside. My video barely kept up with the dark gray figure that flew by. The other two, Moon and Star, lingered over at a dirt pile playing hunt and be hunted. How I loved them!

Later that night, Reddy and Rodney enjoyed a quiet moment in my yard. Swirling and jumping among the grasses by the gazebo and dining on the bird seed I had filled in a feeder on the ground. I put the gazebo lights on, the soft glow illuminating the pair in a halo of light, safe from the darkness. I will forever remember that evening. The two of them looked so majestic and beautiful. I took pictures of them and labeled them "Date Night."

It would be the last time I would see them like that.

I awoke the morning of May 20th at 5:00 AM to Reddy making an awful noise on the road in front of my house. The sound was bellowing through my open bedroom window with such intensity that I opened my eyes and flew out of bed as if it was a house alarm.

If you have ever heard a fox bark or howl, you know it is a sound like no other. The red fox is very vocal and has a quick series of barks with a howl that sounds more like a scream. Because the fox is smaller in size then a dog, their vocalizations are higher pitched. They can make an ow-wow-wow-wow sound that is very yippy and it is thought these barking sequences are part of an identification system so that the foxes can tell each other apart by their call. Sometimes the sound is called a vixen's scream and Reddy proved to be the vixen as she let loose a terrible, screaming howl.

Although that howl is generally used during the breeding season to lure male foxes to them, I sensed something else in her voice. She sounded like she was in pain. No, more than that. She sounded like she was being tortured.

To this day, I feel like she knew where I was and that I would come to her rescue. I did not know what to think, but I knew somewhere deep down that she needed me. I roused my husband, who to my surprise, ran out of bed and joined me in our front yard to confront whatever was harming Reddy.

We stood on our front steps and spotted her standing in the middle of the road, howling. I shushed her, not fully understanding her alarm. I came down and tried to get her out of the road for fear she would get hit but she would not budge. She would move slightly to the left or right, but her noise was constant. A shrilling, hoarse sound emanated from her mouth in an anguished howl. My neighbor, Phil, two houses down, came out talking to her as well, both of us trying to calm her. But I knew what was wrong. I could see the panic in her eyes. She was calling an alarm. Where was Rodney? I could not figure out exactly what she was telling us, but I knew it was bad. Her family was under attack and she was reaching out to her neighboring packs for help. Then she suddenly ran the opposite direction of where I thought her den was and disappeared.

I did not see them again for over 24 hours. The neighbor behind my house and beyond the trees and brush that separated our properties shared that they had seen a scuffle between the foxes and a bobcat and that the bobcat had injured a fox. I was so upset. Rodney must have met a terrible end.

Another neighbor who also followed our foxy family recommended I let it all go. She reminded me that this happens in the wild all the time and goes without human notice.

I knew that, even understood that, but I could not fight the need to find out what had happened to Reddy and her kits. Rodney was possibly injured or worse. Perseus had not been seen for days. The other three were in a precarious plight as well.

The following day at dawn, my husband and I took our dogs for their regular walk. For reasons I can't explain except to say that I felt pulled by some unseen, innate direction within, I decided to change our normal route. It was so out of character of what I normally would do and involved a street I would never use as our starting point.

As we approached the middle of the street, I saw tufts of dark grey fur splattered all over the black tar. Maggie's nose lifted into the air and then she pulled me hard towards the horrific scene. Before me in the middle of the street was a tuft of grey fur and a baby fox tail. Hideous and macabre. I began to cry. Craig tried to ease my mind with talk about nature and that we are only onlookers into their world. But for me Reddy, was different. She looked at me as a mother would look at another mother—with a deep understanding of what it felt like to watch your child suffer and ail.

We finished our walk and went home in silence. Everything I had done to protect those little ones was for naught. I hated that I could not fix everything. My fox family or my daughter. Why do people and things we love have to suffer no matter how hard we try not to let it happen?

We returned and Craig left for work. I started to wash dishes and stood looking out of the window over my sink, wondering what had happened to the little family that had once found safety and solace in the ring of houses that made up our neighborhood. As I was rinsing the coffee pot I looked out to see a familiar sight running from the back wooded area down the middle of my yard.

It was Reddy!

She ran straight towards my bulkhead and directly below my casement window. She came to the edge and sat. Her eyes wild and pained. I shut the water off and spoke through the mesh of the screen to her below.

"Reddy, I am so sorry. I am so sorry that your kit has been taken from you."

She looked up at me as if she was really taking in our conversation. I put the coffee pot down onto the counter and looked out at her. We just stared at each other for a long minute. I wanted to remember every moment of this encounter. She was upset about her kit(s) and wanted to let me know.

"Sorry, girl. It is so unfair that you lost your baby." My voice was almost a whisper.

With that, she ran off and disappeared into the woods behind my house.

That night, we found the body of the kit that lost its tail. My heart was so heavy with hurt. I did not know which one it was but my angst was deepened by thought it could be Reddy Girl. I did not want her to be without her mother.

The next evening, when the neighbor who had the fox babies last cleaned under their shed, he found Perseus' body. In one week's time, we had lost two of the kits and the parents' health was now in jeopardy. They had only made it approximately eight weeks. Eight weeks of life and then they were gone.

These Weaves of Spring had given way to the idea that life was new and precious and swift and uncertain. The natural world is beautiful and yet very brutal. It made me more aware of my own family situation. Cate was enjoying her improved health, and I was relishing a peaceful simple existence. And yet within this little bubble of happiness lay the very real knowledge that in any given moment, it could all be ripped away. The Spring Weave *taught me that within the idea of renewal and rebirth there is a section of my tapestry that could* be sad and tragic. As nature had stitched her essence into my picture, she encouraged me to find places to soothe my mind, body, and soul. Walking a beach, sitting outside and observing the world, and becoming a part of nature helped to alleviate the pain and darkness of the concrete world. The Spring Weave was ushering in the respite of summer and welcoming the longer days of sunlight and warmth of the season. Rebirth can be beautiful but it can also contain a painful sweetness to it. I had finally begun to understand and appreciate both those feelings and was looking forward to the peace that comes from the transformation that was beginning to unfold within me.

3

The Threads of the Summer Weave

"Life, now, was unfolding before me, constantly and visibly, like the flowers of summer that drop fanlike petals on eternal soil."

~ Roman Payne

The Threads of Hope Restored

By early June, the foxes had abandoned their den and become non-existent. The neighbors and I had assumed they had moved on and created a den in a safe location, far from the bobcat and the coyotes. I looked for them for weeks after the death of the two kits, but there were absolutely no sightings of them. I feared that none of them had made it.

Cate had become increasingly edgy about her health and any new bruises or bleeding gums would send her into a panic. Her platelet count had remained consistent and within the normal range and she was able to go through a regular dental cleaning at her dentist. It was at this time it was advised that she have two wisdom teeth removed. What would have previously been a big NO was now something to actually consider.

Her new oral surgeon requested she get written approval from her oncologist hematologist before he'd agree to remove the impacted wisdom teeth. Cate contacted Dana Farber who recommended she go for a full CBC and platelet count. She did everything everyone had asked and moved quickly to get it all that done. She passed with flying colors and was given the thumbs up to proceed. After everything she had been through, I shuddered at the thought of her going through another painful procedure. But Cate was beyond that and was so desperate just to put all her ducks in a row and regain control of her life again. I was impressed by her matter-of-fact approach to all the roadblocks that appeared before her.

The one thing that struck me as a little bizarre was that we were actually grateful for this procedure. We were overwhelmingly thankful for the chance to have impacted wisdom teeth removed, even though it was a painful procedure. Anyone else would have called us crazy, but what this meant was that she was doing something that was deemed routine. Cate had joined the ranks with what so many others take for granted: the opportunity to experience something average. Once she got the okay to have the extraction done, I saw a more relaxed Cate. I believe that she had been restricted from doing things that were deemed fairly easy for so long that an extraction felt like a victory of magnificent proportion! Many of us would have run from that, but Cate viewed the procedure as evidence that she was getting her life back to normal.

She and her boyfriend, Taylor, began making summer vacation plans. He was preparing to go on a birthright trip to Israel and embrace his Jewish faith. Cate was planning a beach getaway to New Hampshire with friends, and Craig and I were planning our vacation to Newport, RI.

As part of a regiment to return to my normal routine, I decided to become more active and start running again. Putting my exercise life on hold during this time frame was a huge deal at my age. It was a lot harder to regain what I had lost. I was not as strong as before, and my run was more of a jog/run sort of training. Every day, I would go out at about 10:00 AM for a three-mile meditative run. I gave up on timing myself and just enjoyed being outside again and increasing my stamina.

A few days before Father's Day, I was out on my run, about a quarter of a mile from my home when I saw something come out of the woods and wetlands about a hundred yards ahead of me. It left the underbrush and stood on the sidewalk. I slowed my pace and wiped the sweat from my brow. A few of the drips had made its way under my sunglasses and salty water burned my eyes. I wiped my eyes and blinked to clear my vision. The animal was clearly dog-like, but small. As I approached it, I pulled out my earbuds, silenced my music, and slowed to a walk. I could clearly see a familiar form in front of me. It was a fox with a full plumed tail and no white tip.

I whispered..."Reddy?"

The fox looked right at me and sat.

My Reddy was alive!

I uttered out loud, "Hey, Reddy!" With that, she stared, never moving from her spot.

Grabbing my phone, I snapped three pictures of her as I approached. I picked up my pace and ran by her. She was a few feet from me on the side of the road, seated on the sidewalk. She watched me pass. I smiled and continued my normal pace and turned, running backwards for a few seconds. I watched her return to the thick brush of the wetlands.

Reddy was alive and she was letting me know.

That same day I ran into my neighbor, Phil, who also loved and followed the fox family.

"I saw our fox within the brush of the wetlands this morning," he said. "I also saw two light red-colored babies."

I halted for just a moment taking in what he said.

"Did you say you saw two babies alive?" my hopeful voice repeated.

"Yes! While I was walking Lizzie early this morning. They stuck their heads out of the brush and then as quick as that, pulled them back in when they saw us."

"Oh, my goodness, Phil! You made my day! That is amazing."

Somehow a feeling of hope and exuberance came into focus. Life was fighting the good fight. It was not perfect, but it had gems of goodness in it.

The Threads of Ordinary Moments

Days before Father's Day, Cate and I decided to go and pick several quarts of strawberries from a local farm in our town. This was a tradition from my past, carried on with my own children, so we could make strawberry shortcake for Father's Day and strawberry jelly for the year. I was secretly so happy that Cate wanted to continue this tradition.

She and I had got up early and went to pick our strawberries before the sun rose too high and made the fields too hot for picking. We pulled into the large farm that rimmed the edge of a small mountain around 7:30 AM and were met with the sweet smells of the earth and dew-covered plantings. We followed the long dirt road and took in the view of vast amounts of farmland on either side. A series of old wooden signs directed seasonal pickers where to go. My car swayed and bumped along the rough road, past a large barn, and straight toward the back field. With our quart containers in hand, we chose our rows and started to pick.

Both of us laughed and ate a few of our red prizes. The sun began to beat down upon us and the bees hummed about the strawberry plants. As was our usual custom, I would settle for no less than eight quarts, but if the berries were big and plentiful, we'd continued to pick and fill a giant bowl I stashed away for just those reasons.

Cate, as usual, was the voice of reason.

"Mom, I think we have more than enough berries to make the jelly, pies, and shortcake."

"Oh, Cate, remember what Grandpa used to say to us when we picked. 'You just don't fill your container, you overflow it.' That is what we need to do!" I cheered.

"Okay," Cate said reluctantly and continued to fill the bowl.

When we were done, Cate took a picture of us holding our bounty with the fields in the background. A treasure of a photo. Strawberry Fields Forever.

We drove back up the road, bouncing and holding our berries still in the back seat of my car until we arrived at the pay station. The farmer's family working the stand welcomed and enjoyed our jubilant visit. It was so awesome experiencing this day. They fed off of our joy, with no knowledge of why, and we had a lovely conversation with them. I paid for our berries and we drove off of the farm. For the record, it was the most expensive strawberry picking I had ever done!

We made our plans for desserts for the weekend and Cate called my mom. It was a tradition for the two of them to make huge batches of strawberry jelly together. My mom made the most amazing jelly, and Cate wanted to learn and perfect this family jewel. My mom was ecstatic about the prospect of having her time with her granddaughter.

What a gift that day was. I loved the simplicity of its treasure. From the outside looking in, it was just a day to pick strawberries. But to Cate and me, and even for my mom, it meant we had received another gift of an ordinary day, another day to treasure on so many levels. We embraced the basic chore of picking berries, loving their color and their plentitude. We embraced the beauty of the morning and the farming community that had provided our bounty and the opportunity to partake. We embraced the simplicity of making basic desserts and jellies while taking part in tradition. None of these things were glamorous, or expensive, or even all that exciting.

They were ordinary, and we appreciated every second of them.

The Threads of Exuberance

My family celebrated Father's Day with a cookout on our patio. The day was filled with sunshine, laughs, yummy food, and good health. As the evening wound down, we relaxed out under the gazebo. I gazed across the brick patio and through the opening of my outdoor bar I spied something odd between the shelving racks. There behind the hanging stemware was a furry head and two ears! A fox head! Reddy was peering through the opening barely four feet from our seated area. I immediately snapped a picture of her with my phone. I had to have that hilarious picture in my fox gallery to look at again and again!

How we laughed that evening. As darkness approached, out wandered Rodney, Reddy and two small little kits. The remaining family was in my yard. What a night, what an experience. I was surrounded by my little fox family and they were still going strong. Reddy was very thin. Rodney walked with a limp in his back right paw. It would be an injury he would carry for life and be a major identifying factor for me in the future. The bigger of the two kits was a trouble-making instigator. He had a large white spot on the tip of his tail that looked like a full moon when he walked away. Was this Moon?

The little fox was a mirror image of her mom, very tiny though, almost too small. She was very attentive to her mom and then I noticed the slight droop in her right ear. It was Reddy Girl! Reddy Girl had survived!

So many more nights that June were filled with lightness and enjoyment. My family would sit in our gazebo at night and the foxes would come by and play right in front of us and lay in the outskirts of the property. We were co-existing with a growing familiarity between us. The joy of this shared time together was so inspirational for me, and for the first time in almost a year and a half, I felt a sense of calm take root in my body.

When I watched Reddy and her family, or when I gave my light and attention to my own family, I was blessed with laughter. Not a forced laugh, but a true belly laugh. I began to want to do more. I felt a peace I had not felt in a very long time. Judy was coming back. I felt her re-emerge.

I welcomed each of those summer nights as a chance to bring my human family and my fox family together. Sarah and Cate loved to be outside and watch them play and run about the back yard. Several times they'd brought dog toys from another yard and played in the grass with them. How extraordinary this experience with these wild creatures had become!

One week later, Cate had successfully made it through her oral surgery. It was the end of June, and she was feeling better with each new day. Her color had come back and she looked so healthy. Remission was hers and she wore it well.

The fox kits were growing and filling out, and although Moon was elusive and wary of us, Reddy Girl loved to hang under the large crimson king maple tree on our property and watch us. I truly enjoyed her presence and even though she was sickly looking to those who observed her, there was no denying the determination I saw in her eyes. They were very similar to those of my Cate.

The Threads of Knowing

As the summer months commenced, we left the first half of the year behind us. I had begun the final process of editing my first book, *Threads*, and my heart felt light. The creativity that flowed from my fingers and into our home was extremely energetic. I found that I embraced working from home with great joy. My motivation was strong and I was striving for a lifetime goal—the publication of my first book. Inwardly, however, I was edgy. I fed off of Cate's illness and her own anxieties. She was trying so hard to return to her old life and yet found herself more cautious than she had been in the previous year. I, too, wanted us to return to our old life, when my biggest issues had been making sure there was enough peanut butter in the cupboard or fussing over the fact that I seemed to be the only person in the house who could replace an empty toilet paper roll.

We both wanted so very badly for her surgery to lead to full and permanent remission and to put this nightmare behind us. But it was always there, nagging us from the back of our minds. She never let it stop her though. She continually put out applications, went on interviews, and hung out with friends. She enjoyed shopping again and her own creative juices had begun to flow. Cate loved making jewelry and had returned to her old standby of creating one-of -a-kind designs.

I wanted her to realize that she could create a new beginning, maybe not with the same objectives as once before, but one that would allow the opportunity for other doors to open. We spoke often of how we needed to let more light into our lives, more humor into our souls. Our inner spirituality needed to be the forefront of what we were trying to become.

To the external world, we were two peas in a pod, loving life and enjoying the ride. But until we felt the inner-peace we both longed for, we would be stuck in this inward struggle for a long time to come. The new objective was to actually be thankful for this path in our lives. Cate and I had long since started to believe that when challenges are cast upon us, there is a reason for them. And if we chose to be open and allow these difficulties to alter our way, maybe these roads would lead us to a greater purpose. In allowing this concept to enter into our mindset, we were almost always able to find the silver lining. Our pictures were being stitched with fortitude and acceptance that added depth to its edges. Gratitude and thankfulness were the seams.

During this time, Reddy returned to our backyard often and became a regularly expected visitor. Rodney was an occasional visitor, always much more wary of the human counterparts that Reddy had embraced. Moon and Reddy Girl were bonding a bit and getting a little more comfortable with the freedom they were now being given. But secretly I was so glad to see my Reddy. Her smiles from below the window filled my hurting heart with a salve that I did not fully comprehend. I actually would feel her coming before she arrived, as if I had a sixth sense about her. The incredible thing was that she would emerge from the thick brush in the corner of my yard at times when my anxiety level seemed highest.

As the end of the day would approach, I often felt a queasiness in my chest. It felt as if darkness ushered in some form of anxiety. No sooner would that heavy feeling arrive, Reddy would appear. Many times, I would spy her sitting on top of the inverted rust-colored canoe. I loved that pose. It was almost comical. She looked like she was sailing into uncharted waters as a captain on her ship. I would watch her clean and smooth her luxurious red-blonde fur, stretch, and yawn. In her presence, everything seemed to be so much clearer. She had a calming way about her and just seeing her soothed my soul and brought an immediate release of tension.

In the early morning, I feed my pet family in a Cinderella sort of fashion. Maggie and Tobin first, the three cats in succession. My husband always got a kick out of my "chanting" as I would begin with a melodic sing-song out loud "Breakfast time, who wants breakfast?"

My family knows I sing or chant many things, but for the animals, it is our thing. Once I start, the animals would come running and the assembly line would begin. First in line is Maggie Mae, then Tobin, and then in the sequence was my cat, Jameson, and then Sarah's cats, Azrael and Luca. When Sarah moved back home from her apartment, she brought those two with her and here they have remained. But the truth is they have gotten so attached to my house and their fellow animals, it would be impossible for them to leave now.

Once that wagon train of animals is fed, I start my trek outside to feed the koi fish and re-fill the bird feeders. It was a little like living in a Disney movie.

One particular early June morning, I sang my song as usual. My husband stood at the counter, sipping his coffee looking out the back window. Within the last lilt of "Breakfast time..." a fox jumped through the thicket, Reddy, to be exact, and she sat at the base of the shed door waiting.

"Umm, Jude, I think your other dog is waiting, too," Craig said with sarcasm in his voice as he pointed to the shed.

I turned with a confused look on my face only to see Reddy sitting so diligently at the base of the shed door looking straight into the house.

I made a regular habit of adding bread crusts and leftover rolls to the suet and birdseed offerings I put out in my yard. The birds, squirrels, foxes, or anything else that visited my yard were free to help themselves, but that morning I gathered some scraps and went outside with the specific intent of giving them to Reddy.

She ran over and devoured them. It was the first time she'd done that, but it became a regular occurrence. If she heard my singing voice, she came running. It was really kind of funny, but I also knew it meant something deeper. It meant she was dwelling not too far from my home. It also meant there was a strong possibility that the kits were nearby too.

The weekend of June 30th promised to be a fun one. Four friends and I made plans to surprise my best friend Paula with a girl's weekend at the Foxwoods Casino in Connecticut for her birthday.

I left Craig with strict instructions on how to care for all the animals. He knew it was a daunting task but took it all in stride.

"I am not going to sing, Jude. But I will feed them and try not to turn them into beef jerky," he teased.

"As long as they have food and water, I am sure they'll be happy. I'm just the floor show," I laughed.

An unsuspecting Paula and I left for our two-hour trip to the casino to see a Criss Angel show, or so Paula thought. When we arrived at the hotel room, our friends were waiting for her with surprises all around. What a blast we had that night. Around 8:00 AM the next morning, I texted Craig from my hotel bed to touch base and also see how the animals were getting along.

"Great," Craig firmly stated. "They all have been fed, watered, and taken out. How was your night?"

"Really fun," I said. But the need to remind him of Reddy was weighing on my mind. "Can you make sure Reddy is okay too?" I pleaded.

Within that moment of conversation, Craig looked out the back yard to see a red blur jump out of the brush and sit promptly at the base of our shed door ramp.

"Um, sure, but she must know we are talking about her. She just showed up," he said astounded.

He snapped a picture of her patiently waiting. I still have that picture on my phone. It would turn out to be one of the last ones I would have of my sweet girl.

Craig went out and put a piece of sweet roll on the large rock she ate near and walked inside.

"All set," he texted.

I smiled. I could not wait to get home and hang with my entire crew and prepare for the Fourth of July celebrations.

The Threads of Protection

On the last night of June, sounds of screeching and howling shattered the usual quiet. In the early morning light, the next day, I saw Reddy in front of our yard with a look of complete terror in her eyes. I looked down at her from my bedroom window as she screamed her eerie howl at the front of my house as if she was telling me something. I opened the window and called down to her. She looked totally frightened. By the time I got downstairs, she was gone.

That was the last time I saw Reddy.

For months to come, I desperately looked for her, refusing to entertain any negative thoughts about her fate. All other sightings of the kits were with Rodney and he had begun to pull away from those carefree visits in my backyard. He spent more time with Moon and I would see Reddy Girl often by herself. I missed Reddy and always thought I would see her again. I continually scanned my backyard for her, but somewhere down in my soul, I knew she wasn't anywhere near. I wanted so badly to know she was okay. I still have no idea what happened to her or where she went.

My heart hurt for little Reddy Girl because she seemed lost. Moon would dive into the ground from a high pounce and nail a mouse or mole with record precision. But my poor Reddy Girl would miss every time. She was awkward and timid. I knew there was a great chance she would not make it past fall. Neighbors who also followed our fox family predicted the same. How could she? She was the weaker of the kits and there was no hope of her becoming a better hunter when food was scarce.

Watching this little fox existing in a wild world that was undoubtedly stacked against her, I became acutely aware of a deep-seeded feeling of protection for her. It was as if I had now become her guardian and protector. I felt an odd responsibility to her mother, Reddy, to help her kit out.

Looking back to that morning when poor Reddy was lamenting and howling in front of my house, I feel there was a deep spiritual connection between us. In those anguished howls, I swear I heard the plea of a mother asking me to take care of her kits. I am sure there are many who would disagree and argue animals do not have that level of understanding, but I was left with so many questions. Why did she come directly to my front yard and look up to my bedroom window? I will always feel that connection and that calling from another plane.

My mind was made up. I would try to find a way to help the furry little waif out and keep her safe.

The Threads of Resourcefulness

The fourth of July brought about a plethora of parties and cookouts throughout the neighborhood. While relaxing outside, I noticed a flurry of activity in the corner of my yard. A little reddish-orange blur of a creature would scurry in and dig, drop, and bury and then leave immediately for another stash.

It was Reddy Girl!

This little ingenious fox was running from one party to another, grabbing what she could and rushing back with her fare to bury in my yard. Ears of corn, chicken bones, watermelon rinds, hamburger buns, and all sorts of sides. She would either eat them in my yard or bury them for later. I had a garbage heap of odds and ends that I would have to pick up every morning. There were scraps of food and tin foil for the next few days but I didn't mind. The only thing that irked me was the corn on the cob ears that were left in heaps. I had to laugh because it was clear she hated corn on the cob. So many ears on the ground and not a single one touched. She might not be a great hunter, but was certainly resourceful and knew how to get her fill of food!

Resourcefulness is defined as "the ability to find quick and clever ways to overcome difficulties." That was Reddy Girl to a "t." It also describes my daughter, Cate. In times where treatments and disappointments were a constant in her life, she continued to find ways around them. Always fighting the obstacles with perseverance, grace, and ability to find humor in the trials. Both of these two kept me in check. They prevented me from riding the pity train and giving into the feeling of despair.

July came to a bittersweet close. I still believed and hoped I would see Reddy again, but in my inner heart I knew I may not. She had gone missing before; maybe this was one of those times? Deep down, I think I knew she wasn't coming back.

I relished those wonderful, carefree days but knew they could not last forever. I wanted to remain in the warmth, peace, and quiet of this time of year and heal my inner wounds. Summertime was filled with visits to the beach and sitting outside in our lovely backyard. My koi pond was teeming with life—fish and frogs lived within its waters, plants flourished, and wildlife visited frequently for a drink.

For a very short time, I felt more at peace than I had at any other time in my life. I was incredibly grateful for it. I embraced this time of ordinary and welcomed it with open arms.

The Threads of One More Day of Normal

Cate remained in remission. Her platelet count held stable for almost six months. Our entire family felt renewed. Summer, it seemed, had brought feelings of promise and hope along with its tan lines and strawberry jelly.

One day in mid-August, I was getting ready for our vacation to Newport, RI. Cate and her boyfriend, Taylor, had a big weekend planned as well.

To celebrate Cate's birthday, Taylor had chosen an outdoor concert at the Xfinity Center in Hartford, CT. He booked a hotel for that night and then planned a trip to Elizabeth Park the next day. Cate was particularly interested in seeing Elizabeth Park, America's oldest rose garden. She had read and learned so much about it that it had become an item on her bucket list for that summer. The weather was gorgeous, sunny and warm, with the blue ceiling of the sky an endless azure color.

The melodic sounds of the birds outside and the hum of my ceiling fan wafting softly above lulled me into a trance. I stood at my bed, folding laundry to pack for our trip and a gentle warm breeze swayed my lace curtains. Cate was also packing her things and I could hear her pacing in her bedroom. My first thought was that she was just excited about her getaway, but something nagged at my inner core. I tried to displace the fear that lingered in my chest. I felt the ominous grip of uncertainty. It was something about the sound of the pacing—the constant creak and moan of the floorboards—that made me feel it was not excitement at all but rather angst and nerves.

I heard Cate in the doorway of my room. I looked up and smiled. She had, understandably, become a tad paranoid these past months of remission. The fear of the floor dropping out from underneath her after the success she had been experiencing was constant. She wanted so badly for it all to be real and not just some kind of fairytale dream inside the nightmare of her disease.

We had tried many times to alleviate that worry and assure her that she had come through the worst of it, but she was plagued with a level of anxiety I did not fully understand. I had just recently attended her yearly physical with her primary care physician. We talked extensively with him about her overwhelming stress and sense of doom. He tried to reassure her that based on all of her blood work and consistent numbers over the past four months, she was doing very well and had no real reason to worry.

After the examination, he took time out to sit down with her and not only discuss her physical health but her mental health as well.

He said, "Cate! You sailed through this physical with flying colors! I think it is time you just relax and try to enjoy life for a change. You know you can call me anytime if you ever begin to experience the same symptoms as before. If you do, I promise we will put through an immediate blood draw."

How I wished she could do as he suggested, but the reality of it all was that she had been through so much that another disappointment I was sure would push her past the edge of what she could handle.

Cate called to me from the door. "Hey Mom."

"Hey Cate," I said, motioning for her to come in. "What's up?"

She looked tired, more from worry I thought, than from illness. Or at least that was my hope.

"I haven't been feeling right and decided to call Dr. J. and have him run a platelet count. They booked it for tomorrow at noon, which means I would have had to come back this way before going to Elizabeth Park. I knew I would feel better if I got it out of the way today, before I go, so I actually went down this morning and had it done."

I looked surprised. She'd handled it all so matter-of-factly. I wasn't sure if I should be worried or impressed.

"Good thinking," I said. "That way you can relax for your concert and the rest of your trip." I was so sure she was overreacting.

Cate smile was forced. "Yeah, I saw Dr. J. in the hallway and he gave me a high five as I walked by. He told me not to worry."

I felt an uneasiness that I had not felt in quite a while. I had become accustomed to this normal life and I liked it. But suddenly I understood her concern.

"Brace yourself," I whispered under my breath, my thoughts slipping through my mouth and out into the open room. I shook my head and chastised myself. *Stop going to those dark places.*

I finished folding my laundry and spent the rest of the day running errands and preparing for our departure and the care of Maggie Mae and Tobin. I did my best to put the conversation behind me and concentrate on the plans of that day.

A few hours later, Taylor came by to pick Cate up and I watched through my bedroom window as they loaded the car with their suitcases, talking, and laughing. Taylor brings a level of levity to every situation and makes Cate belly laugh. It is one of the things I love the most about their relationship.

With the car loaded, the two came in to hug me goodbye. I gave Taylor my regular mom-to-boyfriend mantra, "Drive carefully and be safe."

This time, just like every other time, he replied with a, "Yes, ma'am."

They drove off and I returned to my ordinary life of laundry and vacation preparation.

With the laundry done, car packed, and everything set for the next day's trip to Newport, I had started to prepare a cold plate of assorted salads and fruit for supper. The sun was casting its afternoon shadow over the backyard. I peered out the kitchen casement window, a glimmer of hope that my gut was wrong and I'd see Reddy again. By that point I wasn't seeing much of Reddy Girl anymore either, but there was a constant need to pan the back yard and look for her.

I scanned the usual places, within the wooded buffer zone, on top of the inverted rust-colored canoe, hiding in the tall ornamental grasses, or on the slope of our yard.

Nothing, I thought with disappointment.

Craig had just come into the kitchen to do a final check of our to-do list when the phone rang.

He answered and I became instantly aware of the serious timber of my husband's voice. I placed the peeler down on the kitchen counter. My heart started to thump wildly. We had elderly parents who had various ailments, but the worry in his voice was more familiar. Immediately that well-known angst rose up from somewhere in my gut and pummeled into my heart. Dread, a feeling I had worked so hard to control, was clawing its way through my entire body.

"Yes, I believe we can get a hold of her," Craig said with deep concern in his voice. "She's about 45 minutes away. At a concert. Are you sure?"

I knew it. Damn it! I knew what this was and I did not want it to come back. I did not want to tell her. Damn it!

I walked over to my husband and that horrible phone and stared at him. Tears falling down my face.

When did I get so reactionary? So weak? So weepy?

One of my friends, Brenda, had once described me as "a graceful swan gliding along a beautiful lake, looking so elegant and poised, but under the surface of the pond your little legs are going so fast to keep you afloat so no one knows your struggle."

That's me. Or rather, it was me. I no longer felt like I was gracefully gliding along the surface of my life. This time I was sure I'd sink into the depths below.

Craig's voice snapped me back into focus. "So she needs to be admitted?" How are we going to work this? We can't get her there for at least two hours."

The doctor on the phone said they would have everything set up so that she would go through the Emergency Room for triage and then be fast tracked to the oncology floor for an IVIG treatment.

"What are her numbers?" I asked, "What are they saying?"

My husband whispered over the receiver, "19."

Nineteen thousand measly platelets.

This was the life I thought we had left behind. This numbers game.

The sickening reality hit me that ordinary was fleeting away again and in its place was worry, sadness, and constant anxiety. This non-ordinary life was so familiar that I knew what it was the second it began to seep back into my life.

It held the similar drill of hospitalization and treatment, but this time, something punched my heart with an undeniable truth. One we did not want to hear.

The surgery had failed.

She was not in remission.

She had gone through all the pain, dealt with all the anxiety, and blood draws, for nothing.

The nightmare of chronic ITP had come back and we now had to figure out how to kick its ass again.

Craig hung up the phone.

"Call Cate, she needs to come home."

I dialed her number but either she could not hear her ringer at the concert or her phone was off. I immediately texted Taylor and asked him to have Cate call me.

I spun my cell phone on the counter, mentally willing it to ring. Within a minute my phone lit up. I picked it up and swallowed hard.

"Hey Cate."

"Hey Mom," she said in an overly jubilant voice. "The concert is so awesome! We are all dancing and having so much fun!"

"What's up?" she asked. Still not getting why her mother was calling her at 6:00 PM on what should be a perfect summer's night.

"Cate, Dr. J.'s office just called," I said with hesitation. Stumbling a bit over my words, I continued. "Your platelets have crashed. They need you to come home."

I could hear the shrill in her voice, the tremor of the words, "No, Mom. No!"

I started to feel a little woozy, and the pain in my heart intensified.

"Cate, they want to admit you. I put a call in to Dana Farber to see what they recommend, but regardless, you need to come home."

I could feel her anger. She was so unbelievably angry. I braced for impact. Usually, when she reacted like this she blamed everyone—the doctors, the labs, the meds, the treatments—but I was in her line of fire, so this time she snarled at me.

We waited the hour for her to get home. It felt like 20. I knew it would not be pretty. She was devastated. We all were. We knew what this meant to her and honestly, these blows seem to make her more fragile.

Craig and I whirled with so many emotions. As we waited, I packed a small bag in the event they let me stay overnight at the hospital with her. I still remembered what to pack.

Cate entered the house a ghostly shade of white, her mascara leaving a dark trail where her tears had been. She snipped that she would have to pack a hospital bag and that she did not see the reason she needed to be hospitalized.

Honesty, I didn't either. They had released her from prior hospitalizations with platelet counts at that number. But something felt different and I was very befuddled. I always knew when her platelets were low. I could just look at her and know. How did I miss this? Why did I assume she was overreacting? Surely, she knew her body. The only answer I had was that I was so desperate to believe she was cured I did not want to accept any other outcome.

She came down five minutes later and the four of us were off to the local hospital. Taylor and Craig parked the car while Cate and I went inside to register.

This would be her sixth hospitalization in a little over a year. We were pros, for Christ's sake. We basically told them the drill. Yes, we would have the novice who would look at her numbers and panic as if she was about to hemorrhage to death in front of everyone. We would have to be sterner with this medical professional to push Cate through faster. This time we were more proactive with the process and it paid off and she got into a room much quicker.

We got to her room sometime after 10:30 PM. She had been placed in the only remaining bed left on the oncology floor, a room with a woman in her late 60s, terminal, with her daughter sitting by her side. Because the older patient was so ill, I could not stay over in the room, but could sleep outside in the hall down by the lounge. The nurses set me up in a recliner under a frigid air conditioning vent next to a coffee maker and microwave. A very popular and busy section of the floor, which meant there would be little sleep ahead for me.

Craig and Taylor said their goodbyes and I took the pillow, blanket, and rubberized bottom socks they offered to get me through the night. The floor nurse escorted me down the hall to set up my bed. I unfolded my sheets, added the pillow, took off my shoes, and placed the hospital socks on my feet. I grabbed a cup of coffee and took a sip to help jolt my body into preparedness for the long night ahead. For a few moments, I sat on the recliner and stared out the bank of windows to the array of city lights before me.

I sighed.

Warm, salty tears ran down my face. I wiped them away and sighed again. I knew I was breaking. I could feel my resolve ebbing away. I lectured myself in the silence of my head. *Stop acting like a baby! Stop losing control!* But it was no use. I knew in that instance that my strength was gone. I wanted to be strong. God, I wanted to be, needed to be. Everyone who knew me always remarked about how strong I was, what an incredible mother I was. I actually chuckled to myself and thought how insane that view was right now. Part of me wanted to run away. I wanted to go back in time and be little again and have my mom and dad take care of everything.

The floor nurse must have noticed my sinking resolve and gave me some space before coming over to check on me. The nurses were always awesome on this floor. The most compassionate and dedicated nurses I have ever encountered.

"Can I get you anything?" she asked.

"No, thank you," I replied with a smile. "Well, just one question. I promised her I would keep checking in on her throughout the night. Is that a problem? I was going to go back and make sure she was okay."

"Of course, no problem," she replied with warmth. "I can get you a small chair to sit by her side for a while."

I nodded. "That would be great."

We walked down the hallway together in the dim lights by the patients' rooms, the beeping of the machinery keeping watch over the sick bodies they monitored.

Here we were again.

I hated it. For everyone, but especially for my girl. At just 25, she was too young to be surrounded by death.

As I walked down that endless hallway, I continued my internal lecture. *My God, Judy, keep it together, you can't slip now. You need to keep going. She can't see you slip, not even once.*

I walked in silence alongside the nurse. We reached the outside of Cate's room. I just wanted her to know I would check in with her throughout the night and that I would not be far. I wanted to give her a sense of peace.

My mind was just as tired as my body. I was so emotionally drained inside that I was afraid if I closed my eyes, I would fall into a sleep that would last 1,000 days. My warrior's fighting spirit was shrinking. I was growing weak and I did not like it.

I inhaled and exhaled loudly, pushed my shoulders back, and rounded the corner into her room.

As I entered, she smiled at me, but her eyes were wet. She had set up her laptop with a Netflix show and put the earbuds into the port. She was ready for her night. I sat by her, poured some ice water and handed her a cup.

"Hey Cate. How's it going? Got everything you need?" I questioned with a positive tone in my tired voice.

"Yes, thanks," she whispered.

Large droplets of tears began to roll down her cheeks.

Then she covered her thin face with her petite hands, the sobs growing in intensity. Her body, so fragile, shook with each breath.

"What is wrong, Cate?"

I sat on the side of her hospital bed and stroked her soft strawberry blonde hair.

"Why did I have my blood drawn today?!?" Cate uttered with venom on her tongue. "Why didn't I just do it tomorrow?"

I sat back in complete astonishment.

"What do you mean? You did it because you know your body. You did it because something wasn't right. What difference does it make if you did it today or waited until next week?" I spoke with thick emotion. "Your platelets have crashed, they most likely would have been worse had you waited. Nothing would have changed this outcome."

Cate looked at me with large dark eyes and said blankly, "But I would have had one more day of normal."

That statement blindsided me like the rush of a freight train barely missing the tip of my nose. I felt every single emotion between us. I knew the logistics of her being in the hospital was so very necessary for her care. I knew that this platelet issue had not disappeared and left her alone. I knew, as her mother, how very important it was to keep her safe from strokes, brain bleeds, and hemorrhages. But I never once considered her view of normal. I never realized until that very second that normal for a 20-something was concerts, dinners out, careers, and endless possibilities, NOT weekly visits to cancer centers, treatments, and physical discomfort.

I hugged her and cried with her until she settled down. Then I walked back to my recliner in the lounge and got under the blanket. The clock read 2:35 AM. Normal had left the building.

The Threads of Connection

We were all finally back at home after several days in the hospital, exhausted from working out treatment plans with Dana Farber and D'Amour Cancer Center. I desperately needed a respite from everything and to dedicate some much-needed "me time" to writing and finishing up my *Threads* manuscript. For the first time since Cate's diagnosis with ITP, we were faced with a conflict between the treatment plans.

Dana Farber, her primary caregiver, was pursuing one type of treatment, while D'Amour wanted another. We had to sit down and really understand what was being laid out before her, while walking a tight rope so that we did not alienate either institution. We were beyond stressed and I needed some alone time to sit in my gazebo, among my gardens and my fishpond. The sounds of that beautiful mecca of peace and tranquility were just the medicine I needed.

I decided to seek the cathartic nature of my journal. Journaling had become even more addictive during those days. Cate had given me a new journal for Mother's Day with a fox on the cover and I decided this would be my Reddy Girl journal. I carried it with me almost everywhere and would jot down random notes and moments within its pages.

Dusk was approaching so I walked out with my journal, laptop, and bottle of water. Although evening usually gave a reprieve from the humid heat of the day, that night was sticky and muggy. I decided to sit outside anyway. It was about 8:30 PM and the sun had dipped below the treetops, illuminating the sky with a fierce orange yellow. It gave the impression that the treetops were on fire. How I loved that spiritual visual!

As the daylight faded, my gazebo lights came on and the whole patio was illuminated in a firefly light display with its twinkling white lights, illuminating a great portion of my yard. I was busy typing away on my laptop using my journal as notes, detailing the visual of Reddy Girl in all her splendor from some of my summer memories. I described every nuance and color of her body and face, including the way she sat and looked at me. I felt a connection, almost as if she was nearby.

Inside the house, I heard my dogs' frantic barking through the glass atrium door. I turned to try to spy the object of their panic.

I could hardly believe it. Reddy Girl sat in her favorite spot, under the crimson maple tree looking every bit of how I had just described her. I could not help but smile!

I believe as I detailed that description of Reddy Girl, she was doing the same of me! It was as if the image I created in my head had come to life. What an amazing, powerful moment!

I knew at that very moment, we were connected. Art had come to life and she was not simply a being described in black and white lettering anymore. She was real, and she was before me as flesh and bones. How did this relationship take form and grow? Why did she pick me to co-exist with? What was it between us that linked us to one another? All of these questions were a flurry in my mind. She was like a figment of my imagination come to life to provide solace and comfort. Whatever she was, I was grateful for her and for the first time in several weeks, my heart felt a moment of peace and contentment.

The Threads of Realization

During the weeks that followed Cate's most recent hospitalization, I felt like I was coming apart. It was akin to a completed puzzle that was losing pieces, the remaining picture turning into a shambled mess. Every night as the daylight ebbed into dusk, my anxiety would grow. It was as if something inside me would overtake my mind and possess me with nothing but dark and unhappy thoughts. I would pray for something to redirect my despair and give me hope.

I felt incredibly alone. And scared.

I was surrounded by family and animals, but my angst would get the better of me. I would inwardly talk myself down, but my heart raced and I couldn't shake this weighty feeling of doom.

I viewed the uncontrollable nature of Cate's illness with a form of despair I had not ever felt before. The harder I tried to hide it or bury it, the fiercer it would resurface and take me over.

As a beacon of spiritual warmth, Reddy Girl would come from the shadows of the darkness like a spirit and sit by my window as if she was the calm in the night that came to share the message that I was not alone. I knew it was wrong to encourage her visits, but my need for her life force was inescapable.

I can't be sure when I realized the connection between my sightings of Reddy Girl and the heartbreaking angst I was experiencing with Cate. But as the days progressed, her sightings would ease my pain. As a mother desperate to find a cure for my daughter, I guess I chased any relief I could find. I pleaded at night to catch a glimpse of Reddy Girl. When I did, the joy and excitement would give life to hope and the pain in my chest would lessen.

During the battles that raged between what I was feeling about myself and my ideas about how I thought I should be handling things, I had a fortuitous conversation with Dawn, a friend who was, herself, waging a health war.

Her fight was with brain cancer and she was fighting it valiantly. We were both very grateful that she was well enough to meet me and we decided to meet at a local restaurant. The conversation that day would leave in its wake an incredible message of hope and faith and teach me that you can face anything, good or bad, with the right mindset.

Dawn desperately wanted a life that was deemed normal. Her ideal life was a simple one, one to share with her small family. Having a catastrophic illness had changed all that.

Dawn is a single mom in her early 40s, with two young teenage boys. She works incredibly hard to give her boys a good life. Around the time of Cate's original ITP diagnosis, Dawn and her boys had gone on a long-awaited vacation to California. They were on the Santa Monica Pier one day, towards the end of their vacation, and decided to take a family picture. They were standing along the pier, ocean to their backs, and smiling at the camera. Their faces reflected their pure happiness. A moment of joy emphasized by tanned skin and healthy bodies.

One week later while showering, Dawn felt a severe pain in her back that brought her to her knees. After two days in bed trying to nurse a bad back, she ended up in the ER. There they discovered she had terminal brain cancer and cancerous tumors in her spine and lungs.

The news was beyond crushing. She was forced to face rough treatments and a grim future. She had spent months trying to rationalize how this horrible disease had crept into her life and why it was trying to destroy it.

"I was lying in my hospital bed trying so hard to grasp some sense of reason, of what had changed so quickly that I felt such hopelessness," she shared. "I decided to open up my picture gallery on my phone and look at the past month of my life."

She hesitated a bit, trying to formulate the words of her message.

"I sat up in my hospital bed and started flipping through the pictures of the previous week in California trying to gain some form of strength from the incredible high that was just one week before. That's when I came across the picture of the boys and me on the pier."

I remained silent throughout her story as I hung on every word she shared.

Dawn looked across the table at me with such intensity in her eyes.

"I just stared at the faces in that picture. I looked at my boys, so happy and free. Then I stared at myself as if I was someone else. I was tan and so healthy looking in that shot. One of the best days of my life."

Dawn pulled up the picture on her phone and showed it to me. She smiled and lightly touched the screen.

"Gosh, Judy, in that picture I did not look sick. I stared at that picture and thought the woman in the picture is so tan. So healthy looking. So happy." Her voice trailing off for just a minute.

Then she turned back to the picture and stared again.

"Do you know what I asked myself?"

I knew what she was going to say, but I wanted her to say it. I wanted to hear her words in the intensity of that moment.

"I looked at that woman in the picture and then I looked in the mirror of the woman sitting in her hospital bed. I asked myself, what was the difference between these two women?"

Pointing to the picture on her phone, her voice was steady and strong. "The only difference is that 'she' didn't know she was sick."

I was shocked by the confidence in her voice.

I nodded. It reminded me of Cate's statement that day in the hospital about wanting to feel normal. Being aware that you are seriously ill robs you of happiness and hope. Cate was dancing and singing at her concert even though she had no knowledge of the drastic drop of her platelets. Once she was told, everything changed. The same held true for Dawn.

Our threads melded together in friendship, but both Cate and Dawn shared the ugly thread of serious illness that somehow had stitched its way into their sweet tapestries. Even though I was not the sick one, the one who had to walk the road, I had the empathy and the love for these two women.

Dawn looked up at me and smiled.

She shared that the realization she had while looking at that picture was a turning point for her because she understood that knowing only took the joy out of her life. She was still the same person. But that new understanding had given her the fight she needed to battle her monster disease, at least long enough to be a part of her boys' lives for as long as she could.

Her insight gave me a rush of energy. It renewed my strength to do battle alongside my family and friends, to fight the demons of illness. I suddenly realized that my weakness gave these challenges power and strength. It was easy to feel like the world had been ripped away from me, but in truth, the world was still in my hands. I had just lost sight of the goal.

I do believe that realization comes to each and every one of us at a time when we need to see the truth, no matter how hard it is. It helps us to fight the battles and obstacles that hold us down both mentally and physically. In being able to recognize this fact helped me to armor myself with the necessary stitches that would help hold my tapestry together with steadfast weaves.

The Threads of Kinship

As the summer ebbed away, Reddy Girl increasingly captured my heart. I still agonized over not knowing what had happened to her mom, Reddy, but the not knowing spurred me even more to protect and help her as much as nature would allow.

Rodney came by every once in a while, with both kits and I would observe them hunting together. There were also times when hunting was not the objective. That was my favorite time. Watching Reddy Girl and Moon playing together was a treat. The two would jump upon each other on their hind legs, front paws wrapped around each other in a kind of mystical dance, and then separate and run. There were times that they would hide among the tall grasses and play hide and seek, almost cat-like, and then pounce on one another. There were other times when the two frequented my next-door neighbor's yard and garden. I videoed them with my cell phone jumping over their wire fencing that guarded their vegetables to scrounge and dig. I am sure he must have wondered what had been in his garden, but I never said a word.

It would seem that not much had changed, Reddy Girl had no real hunting skills. She was very inept at catching her prey. Moon, her brother, was much more skilled and Rodney spent more time with him. It was as if this little girl was lost in the shuffle and had no recourse to help her learn to do better. She was great at unearthing grubs and a random mole, but squirrels, chipmunks, and rabbits eluded her every time. I had all but given up on her when I noticed one night, as the last slip of the sun was fading into the far distance, that she would bury her food treasures of the day, only to come back later and unearth them and eat. She had a scavenger way about her and I was convinced that she liked it that way.

Our relationship was not one of close proximity. She never came closer to me than about 15 feet. I liked that. I never wanted us to be in each other's immediate space. I can't tell you my reason. It was not because I did not trust her, but more because I respected her world. I just felt as if I became a familiar companion and handled her, that I could no longer look at her in the same way. I truly liked the magic of our relationship and our separate worlds. I wanted her to remain my spiritual being. If she and I crossed that line, the mystique I carried about this relationship would be gone.

One early morning in late August, I grabbed a cup of coffee and decided to go outside and sit on my deck. It was around 6:30 AM and the sun had begun to chase off the coolness of the morning. I had recently made a point to take in more mornings like this and embraced the solitude of being in my yard with all the wonderful sights and sounds. As I sat in my favorite wicker armchair, legs tucked beneath me and slowly sipping my coffee, I began to recognize how lucky I was to experience the solitude of the moment. My thoughts were completely embroiled in the peaceful mecca of that space when my sixth sense sent out an alert.

Suddenly, I heard a loud rustling in the long, tall ornamental grasses that rimmed my gazebo. The crinkling sound as the lush tall blades began to separate grabbed my attention. There, within all that emerald green, was Moon's little red head staring back at me! His mouth wide open in a strange sort of smile. He reminded me of the raptors in *Jurassic Park* as they hunted for their prey.

I was a tad startled, until I turned to see Reddy Girl sitting under the crimson king, tail wrapped and ear drooped, smiling at me. As I turned back to Moon, there was another fox! A third! I had never seen this one before. He or she was about the same age and size so it definitely was not Rodney. They had brought a friend and clearly trusted me.

I grabbed my cell phone and snapped a pic of all three. I mused for a moment how even with another fox in the picture, my sweet Reddy Girl was still an outcast. My heart hurt for her. I carefully walked down the brick stairs, keeping the three in my periphery. They moved in closer as I walked. It startled me a bit. I walked slowly towards my garage door and quietly grabbed some of Reddy Girl's favorite sweet rolls that I had been saving for her. Continuing with careful steps, I began to scatter the roll in small pieces, but stopped as the three started to rush forward. I smiled and silently issued them back with a wave of my hand.

The three scattered to the upper back part of the yard and I carefully placed the roll, separated into three pieces, on top of Reddy Girl's rock.

Reddy Girl moved away from the trees and lumbered down by the other two. She touted her body with a swagger that appeared to be alpha-like. To my surprise, all three were now sitting to the side of the grasses, about eight feet away. I felt a little edgy, but did not feel at all threatened. As I move back toward my chair, the three approached. Reddy Girl went first and the others followed suit. I carefully continued to walk up onto my deck and waited. I worried that poor Reddy Girl would be overpowered and not get anything. I had held back an extra-large piece in the event she did not get any or the other two became aggressive towards her.

But to my great surprise, Reddy Girl skirted them back and ran in front of them. As they continued to descend down the slope of the yard, Reddy Girl whipped past them again and snarled. She forced the two larger foxes back and began to choose her favorite pieces and munch on the bread. The other two cowered and laid in the grass in a submissive pose. I was completely shocked! When she finished, the other two were allowed to come and eat her scraps!

I could not help but think about how they had alienated her for so long, but that this was her mecca, I was her friend, this was our turf.

She was the boss here. Even though she came with a frailer physique and was not a great hunter, she was smarter.

Reddy Girl was a survivor.

I watched them eat in front of me and then all three laid in the grass besides my gazebo, lolling in the early morning breeze. How intriguing. My little runt had brought her fox family to me and now she was the one they bowed to. I had just watched something truly spectacular.

From that moment on, I understood that they had accepted me. What a victory!

These types of moments continued on and just a few mornings later Moon, Rodney, and Reddy Girl came out of the shadows to join me. I snapped a selfie with the foxes in the background, although it was an early morning shot, and I was just out of bed and not exactly looking my best. I read and understood you shouldn't feed wildlife, so I purposely made sure to make the sweet rolls random and minimal for this foxy crew. This time they had not come looking for food, but rather came to join me as part of their skulk or family. I watched them run and chase each other and stop, cock their heads this way and that, arch their lithe little backs, and leap and pounce.

These mornings filled my heart with joy. I was part of their little group and l liked it. It was an honor and I truly never knew when it would end. Fall was approaching and with that would come the uncertainty of whether they would remain or if I would ever see them again.

Every day was an unknown both inside and outside my house.

The Threads of Siblings

My early morning ritual of writing and editing my book, *Threads*, had become the norm and once the dogs were taken care of, I would find my inspirational spot and sit in my favorite chair and continue my work. One particular morning, I settled in to work, editing and polishing my manuscript. It sounded like the perfect plan except my heart felt restless and my mind wandered frequently. It appeared that my pond was a ploy for procrastination. Deciding to give into it and not force myself into the creative process, I relaxed.

The smell of the early morning dew on the sweet grass was delectable. The birds had just begun their chanting chirps and the rest of the outdoor world was rising. I looked down at my pond and watched my fish swirl in the current of the waterfall. I watched the water lily as it bobbed up and down and float around in the eddy made by the moving water. Several of my fish were feverishly feeding on the roots of the plant and the bugs that clung to it. How I loved this little area and hated to think that within just a few short weeks the warm, summer season would be gone.

I sipped my tea and my mind drifted back to the turmoil that was going on inside my home. As devoted as I was to Cate and her floundering platelets, I was very aware of Sarah. In the past few weeks, several friends and family had asked for her and how she was doing.

She and Cate had always been so tight. When one was down, the other was always there to lift the other, but this ITP had really put a damper on things.

Sarah was always someone who cared deeply, but preferred not to immerse herself in the thick of it. When Cate was in the hospital in Boston for the week, Sarah called daily and was deeply concerned, but chose to not see her sister in that state. She remained at home, taking care of the animals and keeping the home fires burning. That was her forte. I had accepted that of her and realized we all show our gifts in different ways. There really is no right or wrong way to cope when a family is facing a catastrophic illness.

I recalled one time when Sarah was just 10 years old, we had to put our beloved black lab, Corky, to sleep. It was days after Christmas and the whole things tormented both my girls, but especially Sarah because she had gotten Corky for Easter when she was just three years old. They had literally grown up together and the pain of losing him was just unbearable for her. After he passed away at the Animal Hospital, we brought his body home with us to bury in our yard and made a point to do it together. But when the time came to do so, Sarah could not come out. I asked her softly if she was sure and she nodded yes and ran upstairs to her bedroom and closed the door. Craig, Cate, and I went outside and placed his leash, collar, and favorite toy in the grave and said our farewell to our beloved furry family member. Something told me to look back up at the house and I spied Sarah's little head peering out, watching us from the guest bedroom window. I could see the light casted from the hallway behind her, that she sat in the dark watching us, hoping we did not see her. It was then I realized how differently she handled so many difficult things in her life. She would watch from the distance, trying not to be a part of the agony of the moments.

She did the same later in life, at my father's bedside as he was dying of cancer. My father waited and waited for Sarah and I worried she would not be able to come. She entered into the room at the last moment and my father brightened right up and spoke so clearly,

"Look! My final puzzle piece has come!"

And with that Sarah ran into his arms and they sobbed together. She was able to tell him how much she loved him in the privacy of their moments and I now understand how difficult it was for her.

Now she was facing her sister's severe illness and I swear if Sarah could run, her feet would be 10 steps ahead of the rest of her. But she always remained within a distance of her sister Cate.

To say that our family dynamics did not suffer during those sick days with Cate would have been a lie. It was stressful. Sarah understandably felt a little left out and the issues she was dealing with at work or with a relationship never quite compared to what Cate was going through. I tried to listen and give some form of support, but my energy level was near empty and I had spread myself too thin. My mother was ill, my daughter was ill. I was running on fumes.

On a handful of occasions, my inability to be there for her resulted in an emotional outburst complete with enough guilt flying around the room to make me feel inadequate as a mother. I felt guilty for not being there for both of my children in full force. Sarah felt resentment and then ultimate guilt for feeling resentment at her sister's illness. It was perfectly acceptable and hard for her not to feel hurt at times and yet her love for her sister always managed to put things in perspective.

During that time, the only thing I could pat myself on the back for was that Craig and I always encouraged our girls to be there for each other and love each other completely. We stressed to them that people will come and go in their lives, but there is no one who can know you like your sibling. Sharing your origin, your home, and your youth will always bind you. I wanted them to always be able to be there for one another. So far that part of this mess had still held strong and true. Sarah and Cate had remained tight through everything and still called each other their best friend. Knowing that brought such a peace to my heart.

I had just decided I would make a point to do something nice for Sarah and tell her how much I loved her kind and giving nature when the sound of movement in my ornamental grasses suddenly caught my attention once more!

To my left, only about 20 feet away, I saw Moon and Reddy Girl, running about and chasing each other in and out of the greenery. They would freeze as if they were statues and then start the whole process again. It was like I was watching a game of freeze tag and catch-me-if-you-can.

Moon was now considerably larger than Reddy Girl and much fuller. He was strong and extremely flexible in his motion and could switch it up in a moment, suddenly leaping in the air, landing in precision trying to catch invisible prey. I admired his sweetness toward his sister and how they remained together despite the fact that the pack had dwindled. They were very aware of my presence, but I do believe that I was part of their play.

How I enjoyed this secret world.

They ran in between the yards and headed over to my neighbor's vegetable garden. Reddy Girl would stand watch as Moon jumped over the three foot wire fence to hunt for mice and check out the veggies. I got nervous that the neighbors would see him and as I rose to signal for him to get out, he made a mighty leap back over the fence and ran off with Reddy Girl. Then they would return to the front yard and chase each other.

In observing these two siblings, I could not help but not notice that Reddy Girl could not do those mighty leaps and did not have the smooth movements that her brother did. But she had an astute way about her that made her endearing. Although she did not have the standard foxlike demeanor, she encouraged her brother to play with her and showed him how to get food outside the norm. Reddy Girl showed him how being astute can get them food in another way. She included him in her world, my backyard, and he found it intriguing. She was a survivor in practice and in instinct and her brother understood this.

Within these intimate moments, I became aware of the fact that my Sarah and Cate had similar characteristics. And how loving these special sibling relationships truly are.

The Threads of
Thoughtful Reflections

It was the last week of August, and Craig, Cate, and I had made the trek up to Dana Farber in Boston to discuss the next level of treatment. We made our way through the thick Boston traffic and entered onto Jimmy Fund Way to valet our car. Once inside the massive building, we rode the elevator on to the second floor where Cate did her blood draw in the massive lab that encompassed that floor. From there, we proceeded to the eighth floor to see her oncologist hematologist. We checked in with the front desk and waited for Cate to be called.

We chose three seats under an over-sized mural that faced a large bank of floor-to-ceiling windows overlooking the vast cityscape. The sun was bright and the sky a deep blue mottled with white fluffs of clouds. There were so many sick people around us, some from different parts of the world. Those were the times when I was grateful her disease was ITP and not some of the horrible blood diseases like leukemia. Cate and I sat side by side looking out at the view.

An interesting couple sat together a few seats down across from us. The woman was terribly frail and wore a white mask over her face. Although she was there for the obvious reason of seeking remission or a cure, I could not help but look at her face and feel the specter of death surrounding her. Sometimes I hated that about myself, the innate knowing I had carried within me that told me things I did not want to know. I felt compelled to turn and look over at Cate, sitting to my right. She, too, was observing the couple and appeared to feel the same level of pain that I was experiencing.

It was then that I recalled a memory from so long ago. It was as if I had floated away on one of those wispy clouds outside the window to another time period. This memory was so crisp, so clear, that I actually felt I had returned.

It was 1996 and my family had decided to vacation for a week in Plymouth, MA to visit the Plimoth Plantation and see Plymouth Rock. We'd spent the day at the beach and had returned back to town to eat and wander along the harbor. Sarah, six years old at the time, wanted a pilgrim doll from one of the shops and Cate, three years old, wanted ice cream. Craig agreed to go off and shop with Sarah and Cate and I walked down to the harbor's edge to look at the boats and check out the exterior of the Mayflower II.

I remember exactly what Cate was wearing, an adorable lemon-yellow sun suit with white bric-a-brac trim on the edges. A yellow barrette on the top of her head held wisps of her strawberry blonde hair. On her feet, a pair of adorable white leather sandals. She wanted a chocolate ice cream cone and I had cringed at the thought of her pristine sun suit donning splats of chocolate all down the front of it. But we walked down to the harbor together and I bought her a chocolate cone with sprinkles. We sat on the grass along the edge of the water. Cate's hair danced in the breeze and stuck to the sides of her face where the ice cream was smeared from ear to ear. The front of her little sun suit was now mottled with chocolate drops and I was busy wiping and cleaning the drips as fast as I could. I eventually gave up trying to save the fabric and chose to concentrate on wiping her tiny cherub face instead.

Two women sat nearby on the grass. They held hands, not saying a word, their attention transfixed as the sun began to set over the water.

A breathtaking shade of raspberry sherbet began to spread across the horizon.

I watched the two women, not sure if they were sisters, friends, or lovers. One of the women was bald with a red bandana tied loosely around her head. She wore a loose yellow blouse and jean shorts. She was very pale, with dark circles around her eyes. Her friend had short dark hair and wore a powder blue t-shirt and khaki shorts. Save the bald head, I would have guessed they were tourists like me, visiting for a chance to take in the magnificent view.

As the sun continued to descend below the horizon, the two stared ahead, but I could tell the bald woman was crying. I was watching them so intently I hadn't noticed that the ice cream scoop had fallen on the ground and Cate was busy trying to eat the cone.

I looked down at my little daughter and she was very intent on watching the two women as well. I took the last napkin and wiped her face and hands as she placed the uneaten cone on the ground. She looked up at me and smiled and placed her tiny hand in mine and we sat in silence, watching the woman, watching the sunset.

I think we both knew that the woman was sick and sharing this sunset with her loved one. It was such an intense moment that time seemed to slow and everything but the four of us on the grass lawn dropped away. I never forgot that image. The feeling of intimacy within a private moment. In my mind, I studied her face, their hands, and the focus of their moment. I remembered the intensity I felt with Cate and her little hand in mine. It was such a significant moment in my life that I swore I would never forget the woman in the red bandana and her intentional quest to see something so spectacular. I innately knew that my daughter and I had witnessed something very momentous to our own lives, as if it was a premonition of the future, and this vision had prepared us for a spiritual strength that was going to be needed in the years to come.

And then as suddenly and completely as I returned to that day in Plymouth Harbor, I was abruptly thrust back into the present.

"Catherine Cosby," called the nurse.

I jumped and saw Cate grabbing her purse and standing. Craig and I rose and followed her down the hall and into a treatment room. Here we were again, but this time things would be a little different.

Her oncologist hematologist spoke a little differently this time. In the past, it was all about remission and the positive, strong vibe that went along with the potential cure. The goal was to get this done and never have to see him, her doctor, at Dana Farber again. Now it was about finding other options that could possibly put Cate into remission, but her choices were drastically fewer. He expressed how dedicated he was to her and that although the other treatments that she had recently tried had failed, he believed there was one that would be a good option.

He went on to suggest a treatment called Rituxan (rituximab). He had experienced good results with other ITP patients who, like Cate, had not responded well to other treatments. It is a drug typically used to treat Non-Hodgkin's Lymphoma and Chronic Lymphocytic Leukemia. Rituxan is a type of antibody therapy that can be used alone or with chemotherapy and is used to find and attack cancer cells. It is also used to treat ITP and hopefully after several treatments, put patients into remission, possibly permanently. It sounded very promising.

The problem with Rituxan is that it can have serious side effects and some of them can lead to death. Our team encouraged us to pursue it, but to read about it prior to booking the infusion. The medical team was anxious for us to begin as soon as possible because her platelet count was so unstable. We went home and did our usual educate, discuss, and plan for treatments.

After the deliberation and meeting of the minds, we opted to book the treatment to be performed at the D'Amour Cancer Center, a much closer facility to our home. The summer was almost gone and we wanted to move forward. I had recently started a new job working for a local elementary school and school was set to start the Thursday after Labor Day. We booked her infusion for the Tuesday after Labor Day to ensure that if she had any ill effects, I would have a couple of days to help her recover.

The oncology hematology department at D'Amour contacted Cate right away to say they booked the infusion but that it would have to be done in the hospital. There would be a specialized infusion room for her first time doing this treatment and would take approximately five hours. We were surprised by the intensity of this plan, but understood that it was better to be in a hospital setting if she were to experience any life-threatening side effects.

We decided to take a trek back up north to Vermont and visit Craig's parents as a way to try to relax before the onslaught of treatments and appointments ahead of us. Craig's mom was celebrating her birthday and the entire family would be there. It would be a wonderful chance to see Craig's three sisters and their families again. Cate, especially, wanted to see many of her cousins and spend the day catching up.

Craig had gone up a few days before to go fly fishing with his Dad. Sarah had to work and would not be able to join us, but Cate and I decided to take the road trip. We made fun stops along the way, visited with family, walked down to the Battenkill River's edge and sat and let the sounds of the natural world enter into our souls.

That day was so similar to the Newport day in April when we just let our guard down and sat and enjoyed each other's company and the beauty that surrounded us. Together we lingered on the water's edge and listened to the gurgling of the river as it flowed swiftly over the rocks. Within this peaceful mecca of tranquility, we closed our eyes and let the sun drench us in its warmth. The sounds of nature surrounded us with the buzzing bees, the zooms of dragonflies, and the melodic swoosh of the pines.

Although our hearts held a heavy secret that no one from the outside world could possibly know, we had lightened its burden with the salve that day had given us. August was shutting her door and gently ushering us into September and the impending fall season. Summer had brought about much change to our minds, bodies, and souls. That day had given us a gift of respite and harmony and it would be the binding tie of strength and fortitude that would allow us to face the next challenge in our journey. Our threads had fortified and knotted the summer weave and we were ready for the days to come.

Within these summer stitches were the realization of a most coveted thread of the entire weave: The Threads of Being Normal.

These threads are now so respected and sought after in my tapestry. They are the threads that stream within my picture in steady stitches and are a welcomed visitor to it. In those normal weaves, I know what to expect. I know that the joys are simple and welcoming. Status quo, normal, average, nothing special, those are the threads I embrace and savor. The blessings of an ordinary day. That is what I want for everyone.

ৡৣ

The summer stitches were binding and knotting off a segment of our tapestries. A period of change was about to commence and we had little control over its unpredictability. Although we were about to be cast into yet another difficult time, the flexibility needed to go through this challenge was in line with Reddy Girl's innate ability to use wisdom, cunning, and resourcefulness to survive. We did not know it yet, but we would need her qualities to do battle with what was coming.

The summer weave encouraged me to take in the moments where I could relax and find levels of respite, peace, and solitude within the natural world. I do find that many of us take these segments of time in our year and blur them all into one picture. By examining all of the moments that we weave into our days, weeks, and years, we allow ourselves a deeper and wondrous opportunity to see what we have overcome, where we are going, and how incredible we are. The summer weave had inspired me to spend these days with cheerfulness and liveliness. Embracing all of it with an exuberance that filled my being with exhilaration and a zest for life and things like vacation, fun summer activities, or outdoor family events. But within those times of joy, there can also be moments that sparkle with a different shine. Those are the introspective moments, where we are just as happy being within our own skin, relishing all that we have in our immediate world. Recognizing that being average and enjoying a simple existence within the summer weave can be just as magical, if not more so, because summer in now valued in a deeper and more profound way.

4

The Threads of the Fall Weave

"The crickets felt it was their duty to warn everybody that summertime cannot last forever. Even on the most beautiful of days in the whole year – the days when summer is changing into autumn – the crickets spread the rumor of sadness and change."

~E.B. White

The Threads of Reverence

September entered into my picture with warm summer-like days and cooler nights. Nice sleeping weather, as my mom would say. I was always amazed how we could go to the beach at Newport the last weekend of August to find the sand hot and the sun beating down on our skin, only to return the first weekend of September with chilly sand and brisk cool winds. What a difference one week could bring!

The change from summer to fall often brought a bit of resistance in me. I never wanted those summer days to end, and yet, as the fall began to change the color of the leaves and the smell of the autumn weather brought a crispness to the air, I would eventually embrace it as I did my favorite fall hoodies.

Nineteen months into this battle with ITP, we all started to have more moments of hopelessness than we wanted to admit. Even Craig, who had always been the one who could see the practicality of any situation and sort all the good and bad parts into a neat little box, struggled with this. Rarely did he go down the road of emotional reactions, but rather kept to the facts and made it all work.

"This is bad, Jude," he said with despair in his voice. "For the first time, I think we could lose her."

I almost got angry at him. I glared at him and snarled, "What are you talking about?"

Craig looked stunned. He stammered, "I just mean, this time we can't seem to get a handle on anything to do with her remission. She isn't responding to anything."

I wanted to scream at him, "How dare you give up hope!" But all I could do was feel ashamed for making him feel bad for uttering his thoughts out loud.

He looked confused by my reaction and swallowed whatever else he had wanted to say.

I apologized for my reaction. The person who had been a rock for many of us was expressing his heart ache, and I hadn't handled it well. I shared how I felt scared when he wasn't the strong one. I knew it wasn't fair, but I relied on his ever-constant reactions. Finding out that he felt as afraid and unsure as I did, and then hearing him say it out loud was completely unexpected and it frightened me.

Our family slowly started to fracture and crumble. Instead of coming together and working through it with openness and conversation, we all went in opposite directions. Looking back, I think we all needed to deal with it personally, find our own way to come to terms with what we were facing before rejoining and forming our alliance.

Craig was stressed and feeling like the road ahead of us would be extremely difficult and he needed to somehow prepare the family for dire results. Sarah was trying to be a caring big sister and supportive daughter, but she was afraid. She was sad to see her sister go through this ordeal. She desperately wanted us to be the family we were, but that looked like a lifetime away.

I was falling apart inside. I could no longer pretend I was positive and hopeful. A bout of tears erupted without warning, especially if a friend or medical professional asked how Cate was. I would just cry. I did that one day at a luncheon with friends and they were so shocked by my vulnerability that I know it threw off the entire lunch. It was so uncharacteristic of me that even those who knew I was suffering could not believe I would show it.

Cate was trying so hard to not be a drain on her family and friends, but she could not stop this train of sadness. Depression had begun to chip away at her resolve and once that started, none of us could change it.

"Cosby Strong" was the name my friends gave my family team. Even as afraid and hurt as we all were, the distance between us didn't last long. Cate needed us to be a unified force. "Cosby Strong" was ready to do battle.

We talked a bit and decided to strategize how we were all going to help Cate on the next round of treatments. We all accepted that Rituxan was her best option. We booked her first Rituxan treatment for 7:30 AM on Tuesday, September 4th in a specialized room at a local hospital. By that point in our journey, we had grown used to all the heavy duty meds and forms of chemotherapies. Although the side effects terrified her, we were still looking at the prize in the distance...remission.

Cate and I got up early the morning of September 4th and arrived right on time at the hospital. The infusion room team was ready for her and the staff started promptly by checking vitals and making sure she was healthy enough for the treatment. With all the paperwork signed and her vitals stable, they hooked her up to an IV pump and monitor and started the first dose of Rituxan. The key was to start very slowly and with small dosages so they could monitor any severe reactions that occurred. Her vitals would be checked every 30 minutes and as long as she remained stable, they would increase the dosage to the next level.

At the 8:00 AM check, she was doing beautifully and tolerating the treatment well so the next dose was given. I breathed a sigh of relief. The nurses came by at the 8:30 check and verified that her vitals were still stable and that she was ready for another increase in the dosage and drip time. The nurse pressed the various buttons on the infusion pump panel, finished regulating the IV drip flow, and walked away to check on other patients receiving treatments at this unit.

Cate looked good and I snapped a picture of her with her thumbs up on my cell phone and sent it to my husband with the caption "So far, so good!"

I pulled out my laptop and began my final edit of *Threads* while Cate watched a movie on her laptop.

Five minutes later, Cate turned to me and said, "I feel funny."

I questioned her, "What do you mean? What feels funny?"

She answered anxiously, "I don't know. I feel funny and I'm having a hard time swallowing."

I noticed the urgency in her tone and the scared look in her eyes, but the monitor was not beeping an alarm and everything seemed fine.

"The nurse just checked you. Are you sure you're not anxious?" I said trying to keep her calm.

"No, Mom!" she exclaimed. "Something isn't right. Please go get someone now!"

I turned to look beyond our curtain to see no staff nearby, so I hesitated briefly. I feared to leave her alone to look for someone. But when I turned around, Cate had a clear distressing look about her. I chose to leave quickly and hunt down our nurse. Still not locating any staff members nearby, I hurried to the main station desk and demanded a nurse.

"We need a nurse ASAP. My daughter is having trouble swallowing after the last increase of Rituxan!"

The nurses hustled over to her bed and within seconds it was immediately determined that she was indeed in a crisis situation. Her blood pressure was plummeting and a shot of Benadryl was immediately ordered as the other nurse stopped the flow of Rituxan. A crash cart was ordered and a doctor paged to her bed.

I stood there like a statue. Standing and observing, but not believing anything was really wrong. I tried to ask, "What is wrong?" but could barely speak.

Her nurse turned to me and in an urgent tone stated, "Her blood pressure is plummeting." And then she turned her attention back to Cate.

Fifteen minutes from the last time her vitals had been checked to now, my daughter had gone from thumbs up to a critical state. I was so scared for her. The paged doctor and the nursing staff continued to check her vitals, and slowly they began to return to normal.

"She is in the safe zone, stop the treatment and keep her under observation for the next two hours," the doctor instructed his staff.

For two long hours, we waited as they continually checked her and then finally released her after deliberating if she should be admitted to the ER for continued care.

For the moment, Rituxan was off the table.

We drove home, exhausted. By noon she was vomiting uncontrollably and was experiencing severe body shakes. I called Dana Farber who helped me monitor her for the next 24 hours.

In my mind, no one understood this terror. The medical staff responded with a scratch of their heads when it came to why she did not tolerate this treatment. But for the novice in this whole thing, I could not conceptualize what was next. My pain went beyond the obvious observation. My agony came from a place of pure heartache. I was the one who took her home and had to carry her into our house. It was me who tended to her and brought her to the bathroom constantly as she proceeded to vomit severely, shake with tremors, and writhe in pain from the horrific migraine that had set in and tormented her. If I could have ever explained this to anyone, it was that her illness not only took a toll on her and her body but also on those who loved and cared for her. No matter what we did to help her gain remission from this debilitating disease, nothing seemed to work. The weaker she got, the more my heart felt like it would burst into a thousand tiny pieces.

Every part of me knew Cate was suffering horrible, debilitating effects of this disease, but I was dying inside watching her suffer. I did not want it to be about me and yet in order for me to be her rock I needed someone I could lean on and cry to. To burden Craig, who had already expressed his own broken heart, would be too painful. We were a team who bolstered each other, and I needed to share with those outside of my four walls. Someone who would just listen.

It was during this year I learned who did and did not understand this need. It was a painful lesson to learn but one that taught me a lot about some of the friendships in my life. These friends would ask about Cate, but there were so many times that I wished they would have asked what they could do to help me or even just shoot me a text to find out how I was holding up. I needed a shoulder to cry on. I sometimes feel selfish sharing those thoughts. I know there are some who feel uncomfortable with that kind of gesture, or even some who would assume that I did not want to talk about it, but I longed to just be heard. Even a text or a phone call would have made my heart lighter.

Luckily, I did have a handful of wonderful people who understood my pain, even if they did not experience it. They would check in with me, ask me how I was, and convince me to go out and have dinner, lunch, or go shopping with them. It is those people that I will never forget. They were the ones who really helped me and Cate. Being able to step aside from it all and be a normal person, even for an hour, gave me strength to find my inner peace. When I experienced this love from others, my resolve became stronger. Whenever I was able to share my pain or sadness with a friend, I seemed to glean strength. I was able to become more efficient in my duties and see everything with more clarity.

Being able to share with others is invaluable. It allows us to unburden ourselves and sympathize with one another. We are able to learn more about how we are feeling and validate one another. I write this now to say thank you to those individuals. I hope that I will be able to return the favor if ever there is a need to.

Once through the failed attempt with Rituxan, we were now back in a familiar position: playing the waiting game. Waiting to see what all her doctors had in store for her and what the next plan of attack would be.

Craig and I were completely frightened now. Nplate, Promacta, Prednisone, Splenectomy, IVIG, and now Rituxan had not worked. I was looking at the future and it seemed almost impossible. Cate was running out of options as her platelets hung in a precarious balance. It seemed like nature was against her and only her body could decide when to turn the tide.

What came next was not the normal flow of ideas we were used to. Dana Farber did not want to repeat the Rituxan treatment because they did not feel she would be able to withstand another adverse reaction. D'Amour wanted to try again, but this time in a de-sensitizing room specially designed for these cases. There was one at Dana Farber in Boston. Again, we deliberated over the two opposing views. Finally, Dana Farber came to us and said they would try the Rituxan in their facility and that we would have to plan an overnight in Boston. They explained that this level of procedure required an early morning start and would last about 8 hours. She would be monitored very closely and if it was a success, then we would be doing this for the next four weeks, possibly longer.

Cate was desperate to regain her life and agreed. She had lost out on the Rehab Facility job, but was in hopes of finding something similar and closer to home. Because her platelets were so dangerously low, they opted to put her back on Nplate treatments. This would, for the time being, keep her steady until we would could commence the treatments in Boston.

As with Cate's ITP and the variant of it being idiopathic, we were back on the roller coaster ride again. This time on Nplate her platelets began to sore and she was back at a normal level. We never could get a handle on this disease! Idiopathic was the I in ITP and as far as I was concerned, there was no better description.

For now, Dana Farber would keep her strictly on Nplate. In their view, there was no sense making her go through such an ordeal if she was again responding to her previous treatment. Secretly we all breathed a sigh of relief. It was now the end of September and multiple visits to Boston for these tough treatments had already been scheduled throughout the month of October. I know in our hearts none of us believed this was "it," a Hail Mary miraculous recovery, but for now we longed for stable and consistent good health.

Fall burst into life with the autumnal colors that are so spectacular in New England. The oranges, reds, and yellows were in their glory and the air was crisp and cool. Even though fall is all about the leaves dying and the preparation of a long winter, there is something joyful in celebrating the changes of the seasons.

I slowly began to remember a saying from Rachel Marie Martin, "Sometimes you have to let go of the picture of what you thought life would be like and learn to find joy in the story you are actually living."

That was exactly how I felt. I knew this was not what the entire plan for my daughter's life or my family was slated for. We had never entertained the thought of one of our children being ill. But here we were and like a blast of light that hits you straight on, I immediately became aware of what we needed to do. We had to find joy in this journey. Somehow, we were going to have to dig down deep and give our spirits a lift and get the ball rolling. I had been letting fear rule me and the entire family. It was time to change that.

I decided to put my money where my mouth was and find a celebratory gift in every single day. It did not have to be monumental, it just had to be something that instilled in us a gratefulness for life.

I also had to learn to forgive myself for not being perfect. Humans make mistakes. They can be fierce and strong and they can become weak and frightened. I had recently been imperfect and that was okay. Now I had to turn it around again, get a handle on things, and make each and every moment count.

We began to step out of the box of being overwhelmed and began to seek out joy and hope. Cate had a reprieve and we were going to make it a good one. She and Taylor wanted to go out to New Orleans for mid-October and experience some of the wonderful things they had always wanted to do. With Nplate in her corner, we all gave it our blessings. Including all her doctors. Cate and Taylor carefully planned out their costumes, booked their flight and were looking forward to something really special.

I was in the process of preparing for the release of my first book *Threads* and Craig was helping me with the business end of it. Such an exciting time!

Sarah was enjoying life and preparing to celebrate her birthday at the end of October with a big bash and Halloween party.

The acknowledgement of living in the moment and finding joy within the small and big miracles of the day seemed to put a salve on our tired and weary hearts. We were like the trees outside, preparing for yet another phase of life, but filled with the beauty of change and acceptance.

Even in the reverie of living in the moment, I still continued to watch for Reddy Girl. I had noticed that she had become so frail and tiny and I had an innate feeling that she still needed her momma. I became even more aware of how much I attributed her own 'behind the eight ball' kind of existence to Cate.

I believe that subconsciously I had begun to attribute sightings of Reddy Girl to a spiritual guide, like an angel, who could chase away demons and make the dark disappear. Reddy Girl was alive against all odds and although her existence into the winter months was not optimal, I believed she would succeed.

Those who saw her perceived her as unhealthy and not long for this world. I silently became defensive and at times outraged by this opinion. Even now when I think about my reaction, I believe somewhere deep in my soul I was attributing her successes and strength to those of my daughter. As long as Reddy Girl had the fortitude and smarts to survive, so could my Cate.

Both Cate and Reddy Girl came at life with a distinct sass and determination to figure out their next move. Cate never let this tough existence get her completely down and was always up for a challenge. She may have had to fight the demon of depression at times. I think anyone facing a daunting health crisis would feel the darkness of fear. But Cate never let it stop her from pursing treatments, even if she knew they would make her feel even worse, and she never stopped trying to live a normal life. She attributed her faith to a higher power and as long as she had that kind of reverence in her heart, she could beat anything.

The Threads of Wishes

As the October autumn air began to increase in its crispness and the harvest moon shone its brightest, I began to really reflect on the previous nine months. I enjoyed sitting out on my deck in the early evenings as the darkness closed in. As much as I always had mourned the summer ending, I did also enjoy the coolness of the early fall. The smells of wood burning stoves, the rustle of the brightly colored leaves, and the comfort of wearing a warm sweater always put me in a good place.

As I sat very still taking in all of the quiet, Reddy Girl appeared and sauntered out of the corner of the yard. She was more interested in hunting through the newly fallen leaves than she was in me. She looked up several times, but she appeared to be satisfied with just my company and had no real interest in interacting with me.

I heard a noise behind her and a scurry of excitement, and low and behold, there was Moon! He hopped in an arched fashion behind her and grabbed what appeared to be a mouse. I watched him as he "played" with his food before devouring it. The moon shone so brightly that night I could see most of my yard very clearly. Then to my surprise, came the third fox! I leaned forward out of my chair to see if it was Rodney, but did not see the classic bright white tip at the end of the tail, nor the limp that so clearly defined his gait. It appeared to be the third fox I'd met back in August.

Was this a mate for Moon or for Reddy Girl?

I felt very certain it was not a sibling. They ran about my upper yard, leaping, stalking, and playing within the grass. I watched Moon and the new fox stand on their hind legs, front paws wrapped around each other as they hopped across the backyard. I wished I could have grabbed a picture, but was too afraid that if I moved even an inch, they would scurry away, so I chose to embrace this mystical play as a silent observer.

The three of them came even closer to where I sat, and although Moon and Reddy Girl acted as if I was no more of a threat than the crimson king maple in the yard, the new fox jolted if I moved even slightly. It was getting later and I would have to go in soon, but I did not want to leave. I wanted to remain out there with them and be a part of their lives. These moments seemed to surprise me with a more profound learning of who I was and why I was choosing to spend my time watching these little foxes. Then as suddenly as the play started, the three ran off into the woods and disappeared.

I remained in my chair a little longer, listening to the sounds of the night. Ever so slowly I had begun to recognize that I was changing. I no longer desired the things that drew me away from my home life. Instead, I felt extremely at peace with where I was and who I was. I was beginning to trust myself more. In doing so, I could also take responsibility for the decisions I was making, for good and for bad, and embrace them into my life.

Observing these little creatures was teaching me more about myself than any other soul searching I had done before. I was trying to become an author and an entrepreneur. I was caring for my daughter, my mother, and my family. My priorities had shifted greatly and I had been fighting this shift in my life for far too long. My time became valuable and I wanted to choose how to spend it and with whom. I was finally allowing my essence to merge and come together inside of me. I loved socializing and doing great things, but now I had begun to embrace the close-knit world that surrounded me. My inner wisdom was finally getting a chance to grow and have a say in how I was going to proceed in my life. My authentic self was emerging.

Cate and I had begun to relax a bit and enjoy the lull in her treatments. The Nplate treatment seemed to hold her enough to take the short trip out to New Orleans to vacation with Taylor. I had slowly begun to stop letting the disease or the distance rule my thoughts. I was longing for all of us to live a life released from the constant cloud of gloom and doom looming above our heads. I was slowly beginning to trust that God was in control and we had to trust in his course.

Cate's oncologist hematologist had given his blessings and his staff had worked her Nplate treatments so that she could have one dose right before she left and then another when she returned. It was kind of like Cinderella going to the ball and having a great time as long as she followed the Midnight rule. If the clock struck 12, the magic would be lost. As long as Cate stayed within those seven days and no longer, her platelets were guaranteed to hold.

I know she longed for a change of scenery and freedom from her anxiety. I, too, longed for a break. Not from her, but a break from the pain that had dogged my heart for so long. I wanted her to have a life full of happiness, good health, and all the other amazing sensations and emotions that life has to offer. Her taking this trip eased my heart to know she was free to live and enjoy. To experience new cultures and people. For the first time in a very long time, I felt the freedom of ordinary. Even if ordinary came in just a snippet of time, it was ours. My daughter had the gift of a week in a pseudo-healthy state and was going to go on an adventure and smile and be "normal."

Cate did have a wonderful time in New Orleans. She spent the days before Halloween out in the French quarter touring the infamous graveyards, haunted houses, and Marie Laveau sights. She enjoyed the culture and ate Cajun cuisine. She had to rest often, but did so in short spurts and then kept going. I loved hearing her stories and seeing her face when she arrived home. The tightness that had plagued her visage and made her body look so frail was now robust and shiny. Her voice inflection and humorous stories of their escapades made for great storytelling. She presented us all with very thoughtful gifts, but mine was so intriguing. In an antique store, she found an old postcard from the early 1900s of Bourbon Street and an interesting bean seed. She presented the bean to me and shared its purpose.

Folklore required that the recipient of the seed must keep it with them for 10 days, warming it with their body heat. During those days you were to think of something of your heart's desire, a wish. Once the 10 days were completed you were to carefully plant the seed in some dirt and allow it to sprout therefore sprouting the wish.

For 10 days I carefully kept the hard, leather-like brown seed on my person, keeping it in the back pocket of my jeans during the day, and under my pillow at night. On the 10th day, I held it in the palm of my hand, feeling its rough exterior. The brown shell had a slightly yellow tinge to it now. I dug some dirt out of a pot I had in my office with a jade plant already growing in it and planted the seed by its side, gingerly covering the dirt with my pointer finger. I placed the pot back on the end table just under a window. There, I closed my eyes and sent my wish, the wish I carried for almost two years, out into the universe.

No one needed to guess what it was, after all, it was the only thought my heart carried within the depth of my body. I only hoped this seed had the power to make it happen.

The Threads of Traditions

November tiptoed in with a nudge of cold winds and a fond farewell to fall. The leaves, now brown, made a crunching, scraping noise as they blew across the barren ground. The sounds of ducks and geese flying across the sky to a southern location dominated the noises of the season. The days became shorter and the nights grew longer. I reluctantly said farewell to fall and began the process of welcoming winter into New England.

There are things that I love about the month of November. One is that it is my birthday month and therefore is a time of celebrating my life's milestones. The other is that it is the commencement of the holiday season. Thanksgiving and Christmas bring a celebratory vibe that seems to give more value to family, traditions, and spending time together. All good reasons to welcome November into the fabric of life.

November also represents the month of thanks. My heart had become so filled with thankful moments as we had weathered this storm over the previous 10 months. Where we were last autumn compared to where we were currently had brought about such a lesson in what is truly valuable in life. Within this knowledge came an appreciation of living in the moment and embracing who I was. After going through such emotional drama with Cate's platelet crash and subsequent treatment failures, it was a gift to have her platelets hold long enough so that she could pursue yet another type of treatment. Her oncologist hematologist had been more matter-of-fact with Cate's course of treatment. Although it was painful to hear, it was almost a relief.

"We are no longer pursuing remission, Cate. The goal now is maintenance so that you have a quality of life. Medical technology is constantly coming out with newer drugs and treatments and we will proceed as they become available. You've gained stability with Nplate, but we want to now try something different. I am recommending a new med for you called CellCept. It's an anti-rejection drug that transplant patients use. I have patients like you who do not respond to the traditional standard treatments and have enjoyed good results on CellCept. It has minimal side effects. Let's give it a try."

We chose to be grateful for the idea that she had an avenue for treatment and that chasing remission was not on the agenda. The ups and downs of this roller coaster ride called remission had taken its toll. We were going into the next phase of the year with acceptance of a maintenance drug that hopefully would keep her platelet count stable. I was grateful that Cate had the best of the best to treat her disease.

Now, instead of weekly treatments, she would take pills twice a day. Her doctor still insisted on the weekly blood draws for the first couple of months to make sure she remained stable and then would adjust the dosage as needed. Even she looked relaxed with this decision and it did not feel so dark and awful. A quality of life was emerging into her picture and with it a level of acceptance. With acceptance came a level of peace.

I chose to really celebrate the upcoming holidays and do it up big. Decorating became a prime goal and celebrating not just with gifts, but with special traditions and true joy in my heart. I truly became grateful for this year and what it had taught me. I loved being in my home and spending time with my family. The simple joys of watching a movie together or making more homemade dinners and sharing them was so comforting. The more I celebrated my ordinary life, the more I treasured every single second.

Reddy Girl did not appear much during that November and I fretted a lot about her well-being. I would occasionally leave bread ends on her rock and hope to see her, but late at night when I flicked the light on the backyard, it would be gone. It bothered me that she would not show herself. Then I found out why the bread was missing. One night the dogs were barking and when I scanned the back yard area, there near Reddy's rock was the fattest opossum I had ever seen! He was just munching away on that bread having a grand old time. I soon realized this little chubby guy would wait in the bushes for me to place the bread. Then he would waddle out to Reddy Girl's spot and sit like a little old man enjoying his supper.

The disappointment I felt was enormous, but he was so comical, I could not help but get a charge out of the fact he thought I was doing it for him. Even nature appeared to have a sense of humor.

With that realization in the forefront and the fact that the coyotes howled so early now that darkness arrived so much earlier this time of year, I instinctively felt that Reddy Girl was not well and that she may not have survived.

One mid-afternoon, Cate and I went out to do a final raking of the backyard under the bank of trees that rimmed my yard. I spent an extra amount of time under the crimson king maple, the tree Reddy Girl loved to sit underneath and watch us from afar all summer long. It was almost barren with just a few brown dry leaves clinging to its branches. With just a soft gust of wind, they would reluctantly loosen their tether to their branch and then would begin to fall ever so gracefully and relinquish life from the mother tree. There they would lay on the ground in mounds to be raked and bagged. It was especially cold that day and even though we worked up a sweat under our coats and gloves, it was too cold not to be layered up.

I grew fascinated with the few stragglers above, waiting for them to let go so I would be freed from the task of amassing one more pile of leaves. I hated this task as much as I did laundry and was ready to be done with the whole process.

I heard a rustling behind me. I turned to peer into the wooded area and witnessed a very sickly fox walking gingerly along the edge of the yard. Although I would like to convince myself over and over again that it was not Reddy Girl, I knew it was. This fox had the same build as her but was walking very slowly. It sauntered by with sickly eyes that squinted tightly against the wind and light. The fox's head hung low and looked briefly at us, but kept on rummaging through the edge of the yard. It was clear it did not fear us, but was not interested in engaging with us either. Although the fox did not appear to have mange, its fur was thinning and unkempt. I felt so sorry for this creature that must have been so cold and weary and was about to face months of more frigid temperature with a very thin coat.

Cate leaned on the tip of her rake and whispered, "Is that Reddy Girl?"

"I'm not sure, Cate. She didn't respond to me, but didn't run away either," I answered perplexed.

"Mom, if that is Reddy Girl, she doesn't look very healthy."

"I know. Whoever that fox is, I don't think it will last the winter."

The fox sniffed the edges of the property and then continued on its way past the shed, under the canoe and off into the woods. The same path Reddy Girl knew well. My heart was so sad.

The fox disappeared as if it was a specter floating by us and returning to its resting place.

It took me a few minutes to process this sight. To really take it in. My fear had been all along that Reddy Girl's fragility would get the better of her. I did not want to believe that fox was her, but deep down inside I felt it was.

I was putting all of my energy into getting the last of the leaves in the bag and not saying much. My heart hurt. I wanted to protect everyone and everything in my immediate world and yet had absolutely no control over the outcomes destined to be. I could only hope Reddy Girl would survive. I had read that a fox in captivity has a lifespan of approximately 12 to15 years, but in the wild, a red fox's average life span is about 18 months to 3 years. Healthy, Reddy Girl had a limited life-time, but now, in this state, she would be lucky to make it to Christmas. I could only choose to relinquish my worry and concern for her up to God and hope that, somehow, He would help her in one way or another.

I peered over at Cate, still very thin and frail, raking her pile of leaves in a distinct pattern and placing them in the bag. She seemed so intent in the task at hand and finishing the job. She did not have the outward persona of a fierce warrior, but I knew that underneath that delicate façade she had the heart of one.

Could it be that regardless of what your body dictates, if you have the will to fight it all, you could still win?

The Threads of Celebrations

I released my first book, *Threads*, in November and participated in my first book signing the first week of December. These moments of excitement and success were bolstered by the fact that I had my family entourage with me and we did it as a team.

One of the most profound experiences that stemmed from publishing *Threads* was that days after its release, I was invited to participate in a talk with the Young Authors' Club at my town's local junior high. I was so nervous to meet and speak with these 13-year-old authors and immediately felt as if I would be eaten alive. What if they did not like me? What happens if they think I'm boring?

Finally, the date arrived, and I was ready to speak with the students. I had been scheduled to arrive for the last period of the day. There were approximately 35 club members who were invited to hear me speak, as well as some English classes that were interested in the "meet and greet" of a local author.

I found one available visitor parking space at an island just below the left side of the building. I parked my car, I sat and re-applied my makeup, took a sip of water, and proceeded to amass my notes and copy of *Threads*. Something drew my eyes up towards a second floor window. I thought I saw a person peering out the window. I suddenly had this overpowering memory of a young girl sitting in that very classroom and daydreaming out the same window. I was that young girl 40-some-odd years earlier! How I would love to daydream in that room and let my mind wander out at the large green lawn and cloud-scattered skies. So many afternoons I would wonder what my life would be like in the future. Would I ever marry? Would I have an incredible career? Could I ever write a book?

"Oh, my goodness!" I said out loud. "If only your 13-year-old self could see you now!"

I was always shy and never imagined I had the ability to speak in front of people, or even draw a crowd. I had dreamed about writing a book since junior high and here I was about to share my experience with those who had the same dream! It was a pay-it-forward moment in the making and I wanted to make sure I did it right.

Every ounce of my being wanted to make an impact on these young hopeful minds. That day still stands out for me as a top 10 experience. Success is defined in many different levels, but for me, success was that day, in front of those students, sharing my dream and encouraging theirs.

Although becoming a published author is not an ordinary accomplishment, nor were the subsequent book signings or the speech at the local junior high, I did recognize that these moments were part of a larger picture. In many ways it was a very humbling experience. I had not only endured the burden and heartache of seeing my youngest go through a tough illness, but I had also found a piece of myself I did not know existed. I approached that life goal with a great deal of modesty. I chose to believe I was relaying a message of hope through *Threads* and actually helping others to heal and find their spiritual self. In those moments of beyond ordinary, I chose to relinquish pride and accept this gift with modesty and thankfulness.

Thursday, December 6th was a whirlwind kind of day with a re-check for Cate in Boston in the morning and a book signing that evening. We all made it home late in the afternoon and turned around and went to the book signing at a very popular local restaurant, Casa

Di Lisa. Cate was well enough to attend and she and Sarah helped greet people and assisted them with signing up for the raffle prize. Craig did the business end of it and was my organizer. What a lovely team I had.

That night, in that room was pure magic. The reception I received was amazing. It was equivalent to a George Bailey moment in *It's a Wonderful Life*. The room was filled with people who celebrated my success with me. There were people from all parts of my past and present. Some were neighbors from my childhood, others from my present neighborhood. There were friends from elementary school, high school, college, and work, and of course, my entire family around me.

As my mother said, "Judy what a night! You had a lot of love in that room. A lot. Not many people get to see so many people from so many facets of their life celebrate a milestone with them."

How could I deny that? It was true. My year had started with such heartache and despair and was ending with such a beautiful display of love and support. I truly feel like that journey was so life changing and created a design that was so vibrant in my tapestry in both depth and width. I can only imagine that within that year there were so many gold and silver moments. Rare moments that made my tapestry so beautiful and precious and glitter with magic.

Our Christmas that year was to be so different from any other. I did not stress over perfect gifts or perfect trees and how much I could cram within those four weeks of Christmas celebrations. Instead, I enjoyed every single moment of time with all our family members and friends and treasured the quality of time I had with them. Cate seemed to be in a different place, too. She was so happy to be able to just be herself. Acceptance had woven a distinct and formidable thread within our tapestries and we had allowed it to enter into our seams at exactly the same time.

Stability and ordinary were such a welcome part of our lives now and wherever the future took us, this year was a life lesson of what really made us happy and thankful. Ordinary moments within extraordinary times.

The Threads of the Spirit Animal Revealed

As I reviewed my life with my family and how much our tapestries had grown within this relatively short period of time, I began to think about my little fox family too. Once I had allowed acceptance that Reddy Girl may have met a sad end, I also found hope that she did not. In releasing the emotional tie, the almost irrational bond I had with these creatures, I began to see a clearer picture.

Reddy Girl had become so popular on my personal Facebook page. I was surprised how many people wanted her to succeed and enjoyed her antics. In one of those posts, a very spiritual friend stated Reddy Girl was my "spirit animal." What was so interesting about that comment was that it came on a day I had written exactly that description of her. It was a kismet moment and I began to really look at the extraordinary moments of interaction with these foxes over the course of a year. Never had I experienced anything so intimate with a wild animal, and it had happened in such a tumultuous year for me. It was then the idea of the spirit animal tied a knot in my tapestry and emerged in front of me with a clarity that was so profound I could not deny it.

From the moment that Reddy and Rodney entered into my picture along with their four kits, until the intense connection I had with my constant visitor Reddy Girl, it never occurred to me that she may be a spirit animal. I had always imagined the wolf as mine, all brute strength and fierceness. I'd never in a million years have thought of a fox as something I would attribute my spirit to. I was beginning to recognize that under the surface there was something mystical about this beautiful animal. Subtle and cunning, the fox faces adversity with a defined objective. The fox must rely on her sharp mind and agile body to survive.

Using my inner strength as my way to navigate through the difficult moments and relinquish my failing outer strength to a cunning power of determination and overcoming, I immediately felt the connection.

I mused to myself why a spirit animal may make themselves known. Why do they come to us at all? I have read spirit animals come to us at times when we need to be more in tune with nature and the earth, but also when we require assistance in making decisions in our life.

In order to understand this incredible benefaction of the spirit animal, one needed to witness these animals in their natural form. Observation of their innate behaviors and intelligence requires a level of respect. When applying that statement to me, it was apparent that I had enjoyed them on an almost daily basis in their natural habitat. During those days and nights of interaction, I wanted to be accepted into their world and watch them. What intrigued me more was that I never once felt like I wanted to own her or even touch her. I was more than content to simply co-exist within her world. Respect was critical in my observation of her.

The connection of the spirit animal is important in order to understand this gift. Meditation, prayer, or an openness to connect with the natural world is key to being able to communicate with them. I had experienced this on several levels, such as the need to see her and the natural relationship we had when we did meet. Nothing I had done before or since had prepared me for that level of connection. Reddy and

Reddy Girl connected with me through their eyes. There was familiarity in those eyes, as if we truly knew each other on a whole other level.

As she entered into my world, or me into hers, I realized there was some message deep down inside that I tried to decipher from her. But it was as if I was on one side of an invisible wall and she was on the other side with the sounds of our communication being muffled by the barrier between us.

I began to notice that wherever I went I would see fox items. I posted pictures on Facebook and Instagram of my interactions with her and soon discovered she had a social media following. A positive following. It was incredible. People began sending me gifts of fox items and I suddenly understood that she was a constant reminder in my life.

It was then that I began to recognize a deeper meaning between us. I needed to honor her, to understand and appreciate that she picked me, not the other way around. I realized that with this relationship, although seen by some as out-of-the-box thinking, I only knew what was arising from within me. I needed to decipher what she was telling me and let her know I was finally ready to receive the message. There was an inner understanding that these messages would not come straight forward, but rather be relayed through a series of meetings and events. It was up to me to read her, to hear her, to understand her. I obviously was not ready yet, but I knew as long as Reddy Girl came to visit and sit under the red maple tree and dwell within my world, I would never stop trying to heed her message.

꙳

The Threads of the Fall weave were finishing their final knots and embellishments on our tapestries. Within these sections of our masterpieces were designs filled with beautiful moments forged with fortitude, faith, hope, and acceptance. We were slowly relinquishing control of the unknown and allowing it to create a new dimension within our tapestry. The reverence of our higher power was now the strongest binding stitch. These strands are available to all who believe and trust in a greater vision, and understand that although the road may not be an easy one, it is one filled with moments and experiences that will always enrich our lives. I had finally become open and accepted these times of our lives with humility and love. As my family and I continued on the difficult path that we were given, we tried our hardest to persevere and do our best, no matter the trial. *I now believe that in showing reverence and gratefulness, my family and I have been allowed a sense of grace, and above all, peace of heart.*

5

The Threads of the Final Weave

"An invisible red thread connects those who are destined to meet, regardless of time, place, or circumstance. The thread may stretch or tangle, but will never break."

~Ancient Chinese Proverb

The Threads of the Spirit

The year had come full circle. As the cold winds of the north returned to the landscape and the final leaves had fallen from the trees, leaving the bare and gnarled bark naked to the world, Reddy Girl stood stoic at the edge of my property. It was dusk and the icy temperatures had descended upon the land. Dark grey clouds were moving in and the air smelled of impending snow. As the last slit of winter sun slipped beneath the clouds, the chill was even more present. I had brought out a few recyclables to place in our container when I spied her standing on the slope of our yard.

All that I could make out was the distinct silhouette of a fox masked in the dim light. I tried to get a better visual, but I really wasn't sure. I stopped and pulled my cardigan closer to my body and threw the cans into the bin. The loud clanking noise that sounded as they hit the bottom of the bin did not scare off the fox. I instantly had the urge to run and get her favorite sweet rolls and throw them to her, but I was not one hundred percent sure it was her.

I yelled into the icy breeze, "Reddy Girl, is that you?"

The fox shifted a little and ran back into the darkness of the next yard. I called again, with the familiar clicking noise I had used before, "Reddy Girl, want some bread?"

All I could see was the red glint of eyes in the duskiness.

Why would she be afraid of me? Why is she distant? Is that her?

I quickly ran through the garage door and into my kitchen where I grabbed the bag of rolls and returned outside.

As I threw the bread down into her familiar feeding spot I softly whispered once more, "Reddy Girl..."

Suddenly there was movement in front of me. At the edge of the darkness from where my back light would cast its beacon, stood the fox. It remained stationary, still shadowed in darkness.

"Hey, girl! You need to eat up, for food is going to get scarce for you my friend."

With that, she edged into the light and sat, her now-full, thick tail wrapped around her bottom. Her classic move. Then while sitting, she cocked her head, leaving the right ear to droop.

I smiled. It was her. All grown up. She had made it against all odds. She knew enough to fear the human, but was smart enough to know where she could get a bite.

My girl had made it.

I stood across from her as she scurried into the light and grabbed her bread and chewed. Her soft brown eyes were now fully locked on me. I could not help but relish this moment between us. I had been honored by her trust and her friendship. There is something so very special about being in her presence. I was allowed to share a part of her life and witness it from a very sacred place. She was so much like my Cate—strong, resilient, and undeniably astute. Even against all odds, they both found their way. I breathed the frigid air into my lungs and exhaled. I wanted this moment to last forever. She ate the bread quickly and sniffed the ground around for extra crumbs.

"Hey girl, how have you been? Where have you been?"

She looked up and sat. Sometimes she could appear so cat-like. I could not help but notice her eyes. They had softened in this brief exchange. She looked so much like her Momma. She was much smaller and her face was still pup-like, but the way her eyes smiled was just like her mom.

I uttered, "Be safe, Reddy Girl."

She ran into the duskiness of my back yard, sat, and began to scratch quickly behind her right ear. In the middle of a scratch, she stopped and looked at me one more time. Within in that singular moment, Reddy Girl turned into the darkness and ran beyond the wooded buffer zone. The moon could not illuminate the inky blackness of the spot where she was enveloped into its mystical veil.

I stood still, listening for sounds of cracking sticks or rustling leaves, but she had moved away with stealth and quiet. I knew I would most likely not see her until spring and there was a great possibility, I would never see her again. I felt a salty tear slip from the corner of my eye. Turning from the cold outside world, I entered into the warmth of my home.

I knew in that instant who she was and why she had come by one last time. She was my spirit animal. My muse, my inspiration. I had learned so much from our year-long encounter and I knew at that moment I had to let her go. I had to give it all up to God and believe that all those I love and cherish will be protected and guided by him.

&〜〜

The gift of the Threads of the Spirit is to believe that in every stitch that is placed within our tapestry, it has a divine hand guiding it along. Although the paths and choices we opt to follow may be of our own design, it is with His loving hand that we are able to stitch our worries and burdens with steadfast faith. In giving it up to God and praying for His assistance, our tapestry's picture is forever forged with ethereal designs and guidance.

We were all "ready" to embrace our journey.

Epilogue

"We look at life from the back side of the tapestry. And most of the time, what we see is loose threads, tangled knots and the like. But occasionally, God's light shines through the tapestry, and we get a glimpse of the larger design with God weaving together the darks and lights of existence."

~ John Piper

One early spring night, I heard the next door neighbor's dog howling in a frantic sort of way. I was sitting in my living room watching TV and suddenly "felt" Reddy Girl. It was as if I could sense that she was frightened and needed to be helped. I had not seen her in almost three months and had assumed she had moved on, but then a sixth sense feeling began to emerge from within me.

I turned on the back lights and scanned the yard intensely. My own dogs were barking, partly from the alarm barks from next door, and the other part because they knew what I was doing. They knew I was looking for her...the wild beast that mommy liked.

I spied her cowering in the corner of the yard, obviously not sure what to do. I spoke softly to my husband. "She's here."

I slowly walked through the kitchen, tiptoed out the side door, and exited through the back garage door. I called to her with my clicking noise.

"Reddy Girl. It's okay."

To my great surprise, she bolted straight for me, running through the darkness, over the incline and down through the brick patio. I startled for a moment, which, in turn, scared her.

"Reddy Girl, what are you doing? You're okay, no one is going to hurt you. Do you want something to eat?"

The fox looked at me with almost pleading eyes. I had to laugh to myself. I could imagine her looking at me and answering in her little voice, "Why yes, Judy. What do you think?"

"I'm insane." I muttered under my breath and turned slowly to go into the house to retrieve some old bread ends but wished I had her favorite sweet rolls. As I entered back into the kitchen my dogs were in full bark mode, lecturing their master for her careless behavior.

Craig was standing in the kitchen. "Did you see how fast she came running towards you? That was wild!"

I smiled. "Yes. For a split second, I was scared. But then I knew it was her."

He laughed. "Of course it's her! No other fox would come to you like that."

I went back outside and found her sitting next to the tall ornamental grasses. I threw the bread, but the breeze suddenly took the pieces and they scattered right next to our trash cans. Reddy Girl came over to the cans and grabbed a piece but skittered this way and that way, obviously frightened by the movement they made in the swaying wind. She ran under our red bud tree and sat, debating whether she really wanted to eat or run.

I edged closer and picked up the bread, and this time placed it in her normal spot, right on her feeding rock. Then I did something so unusual for me. I knelt down on the moist evening ground.

Reddy Girl scurried over, body language showing a calmer demeanor. It suddenly occurred to me that she trusted my presence. I made her feel safe and she liked that.

I stayed very still, aside from the breeze blowing my long curly hair about my face. She edged closer, only about two feet away from me and began to chew. I was eye level with her. I could see her beautiful soft brown eyes, her mouth curled in a smile, her fur, thickening in parts, thinning in other sections, blowing in the wind, and her beautiful black stocking legs.

There we were, face to face.

My heart was racing. The exhilaration was palpable. This was pure magic and I was gifted with some sort of spiritual connection with this beautiful animal.

I did not ever feel she would harm me, although I heard the multitudes in my head telling me how I was incredibly careless to be this close to a wild animal. Instead, I felt this immediate feeling of mutual respect and binding of our worlds. The seams of our tapestries were finally weaving together in perfect harmony. The wind caressing our bodies, the smells from the earth entering our nostrils, and the imagery of our eyes locked on one another for a brief moment in time were bound by a higher power. I whispered to her,

"Thank you, Reddy Girl. Thank you for being a part of my year and teaching me it will all be okay."

Reddy Girl looked at me with knowing eyes and continued to chew her bread pieces.

I continued, "I know who you are. What you are. You are my spirit animal. I hope I see you again."

I suddenly felt a strong pang of sadness for her mother, Reddy. If it were not for all those times she had reached out to me, I would never have let my guard down or allowed myself to be open to this intense experience. Although the path was designed so that I could know her daughter and become her protector, there was a greater message in Reddy's ultimate sacrifice. A message of the love of a mother for her child.

I wish I could have lingered longer, but she was startled from noises made by the wind and scurried away into the darkness again. Even when I look back and think of that moment, I knew there was a greater purpose to that interaction, but I was not savvy enough to recognize it all. Even in this intimate moment, I still never imagined reaching out to touch her soft head or caress her back. That would have felt so wrong. It was not a fear of getting bitten or of an attack, but more of a feeling like I was not worthy.

It hit me in the most profound way because I realized later that evening how much I loved the simplicity of that moment. It was so wonderful just to be in my own skin with a creature who would not judge me for my looks, smarts, material things, career choices, or popularity. Our connection was based solely on our inner beings, our souls. What a wonderful feeling to be that comfortable with something. To be able to recognize that all that was between us was trust and our beautiful essences. I do believe this last visit was an affirmation of our connection and of the messages she had been sent to relay to me during that difficult year of transformation. Her message was simple. She encouraged me to trust my heart, inspire all those I can in a positive way, and continue to follow my path with an optimistic outlook regardless of the changes in my life.

But above all her message was of trust and encouragement to let my authentic self shine.

Weaving our magic together again was a reminder of why her visitations were so very important to me. As long as Reddy Girl was my spirit animal, I knew my messages of hope, faith, and fortitude would always be present.

Message From The Author

Thank you for reading Spirit Threads. If you enjoyed this book, would you please consider leaving a review at the following websites:

www.amazon.com

and

www.barnesandnoble.com

For more information please visit me at the following:

https://www.judithcosby.com

https://www.facebook.com/JudithAnnCosby

https://www.linkedin.com/in/judith-cosby-799079124

https://www.instagram.com/judy.r.cosby

https://twitter.com/cosby_judith

judithacosby@gmail.com

Also by Judith Cosby

Available now on

www.amazon.com

and

www.barnesandnoble.com

Made in the USA
Middletown, DE
27 November 2019